A Brighter Choice

A Brighter Choice

Building a Just School in an Unequal City

Clara Hemphill

Published by Teachers College Press, 1234 Amsterdam Avenue, New York, NY 10027

Front cover image by Paulo Silva / Unsplash.

Library of Congress Cataloging-in-Publication Data is available at loc.gov

ISBN 978-0-8077-6798-6 (paper)
ISBN 978-0-8077-6799-3 (hardcover)
ISBN 978-0-8077-8154-8 (ebook)

Printed on acid-free paper
Manufactured in the United States of America

To Little Keyonn and all the children
of Brighter Choice Community School

Contents

Introduction

What happens to public schools when a neighborhood gentrifies? As a journalist and parent advocate, I was trying to answer that question when my colleague at The New School's Center for New York City Affairs, Keyonn Wright-Sheppard, introduced me to his son's school, Brighter Choice Community School, a Black-majority public elementary school in Brooklyn's rapidly gentrifying Bedford-Stuyvesant. Long a school that served mostly poor and working-class families, Brighter Choice was beginning to attract middle-class and professional families, mostly Black, a few White. Spend time at Brighter Choice, Keyonn said, and you'll begin to understand the complicated dynamics of schools in changing neighborhoods. This book is the result of the 3 years I spent visiting Brighter Choice, from 2019 to 2022.

I have visited hundreds of New York City public schools over the past 25 years, first as the author of a series of guidebooks to the schools, then as the founding editor of the InsideSchools.org website, which offers school reviews and data to help parents navigate a complex system of school choice. At The New School, I led a research project examining racial and economic segregation in the city's schools; we produced a series of policy reports outlining potential strategies for more integration. My years at Brighter Choice were the first time I was able to focus on one school in depth, with dozens of visits and repeated conversations with many parents.

As a White researcher, I am still confronting my own biases, including a tendency to identify with White families and to underestimate how the dynamics of race and class influence even routine interactions at schools like Brighter Choice. In my conversations with Black parents, I discovered how little I knew about their experiences with the school system. I came to realize that delving into the history of race relations, both in the city and in the schools, is crucial to understanding how the educational system functions today.

Keyonn's wife, Keesha Wright-Sheppard, was elected PTA president at Brighter Choice in 2019. As a middle-class Black family, Keesha and Keyonn viewed the school's growing number of White and wealthier families with both hope and trepidation. On the one hand, they felt these families could help sustain enrollments and bring much needed resources to the school. On the other hand, some of these parents made demands that clashed with the school's culture and failed to recognize its role in the Black community.

During my time at the school, the challenges faced were even greater than I imagined. Teachers struggled to reach pupils who missed weeks of school because of chronic asthma or homelessness. A fire destroyed Keyonn and Keesha's home. Neighborhood violence killed the baby brother of a Brighter Choice student. A global pandemic closed the school for months and left a 4-year-child without a mother.

The school community worked to make up for these challenges: The principal opened the school each Saturday for kids to skateboard. Parents hauled a washer-dryer to the school so homeless families could wash their clothes. The PTA organized events, such as a fall festival, to bring parents of different races and income levels together. Neighborhood restaurateurs donated food. Parents contributed what they could, either time or resources or both. It wasn't all "Kumbaya." There were quarrels, misunderstandings, and hurt feelings. But parents were wrestling with the inequalities in our society, doing the best they could to ameliorate them and create an inclusive and effective public school.

There are deep inequalities in New York City's school system: Parents in White and Asian neighborhoods can mostly rely on their local elementary schools—and simply enroll their children with proof of address—while parents in Black and Latino neighborhoods often jump through hoops to find schools, like Brighter Choice, that serve their children well. This book traces the roots of this inequality, the history of failed school reforms designed to address it, and the struggle of parents at one small school for equality and justice.

Chapter 1 introduces Keesha as she vows to build a school that welcomes well-off newcomers while ensuring that lower-income families continue to have their voices heard.

Chapters 2 to 5 tell the history of Brooklyn's schools from the 1950s—when redlining and disinvestment starved Bedford-Stuyvesant of resources—to the 2000s—when Mayor Mike Bloomberg's expansion of school choice offered children new opportunities but left most traditional schools in Bedford-Stuyvesant with declining enrollments and low levels of achievement.

Chapters 6 to 10 tell how Keesha, together with other parents, the principal, and staff at Brighter Choice worked to build a community across the great divides of race and class. It's an unfinished story, with many setbacks, but an optimistic one.

In cities across the United States, affluent White newcomers are moving into historically Black, low-income neighborhoods, presenting both a challenge and an opportunity for public schools. In many cases, the newcomers avoid their local schools. In other cases, the newcomers use their political power to shape the schools in ways that ignore the needs of families who have lived in the neighborhood for years. In both circumstances, entrenched inequality remains. But there's a third possibility, one that can bring greater equity, and that's the one that gave Keesha hope.

ONE

A Proudly Black School in a Gentrifying Neighborhood

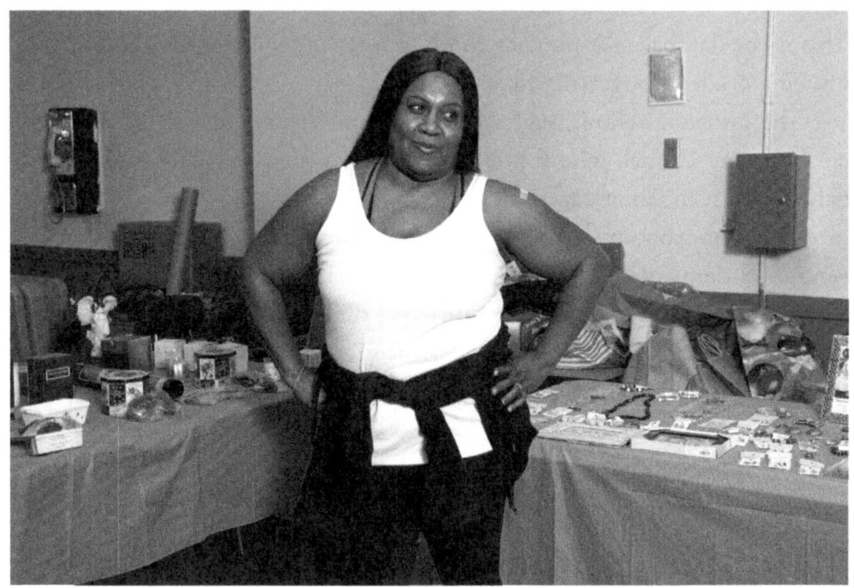

Kristina Bumphrey/Kristina B. Photography

"We can learn to speak to one another in a way that's not offensive," Keesha says.

On a hot September morning in 2019, Keesha Wright-Sheppard, the new president of the Parent Teacher Association, wiped sweat from her brow as she welcomed parents and children to a tiny public elementary school in Bedford-Stuyvesant, a historically Black Brooklyn neighborhood that in recent years has seen skyrocketing rents and an influx of White residents.

It was the first day of school. Brighter Choice Community School, like about one-quarter of the city's public schools, had no air conditioning. The air was heavy in the gray-tiled corridor at the entrance to the building. "Man, I've got to get some water," Keesha said to no one in particular.

A boom box blasted "I'm a Believer." Yellow and white balloons decorated long tables with folding chairs and clipboards for parents to sign up for after-school programs and the PTA newsletter.

Keesha greeted parents and admired how much the students—mostly Black and Latino, but including a handful of White and Asian children—had grown over the summer. She sold yellow polo shirts with the school's logo.

"Good morning! Good morning!" she said. "Look at the 5th-graders Long sleeve is $17, short sleeve $13. Sign up for after-school is over there. This is the database for parents. We'll let you know everything that's going on. First grade? Congratulations!"

The previous school year had been a tumultuous one. A White principal, Jeremy Daniel, whom nobody knew, had unexpectedly replaced the beloved African American principal, Fabayo McIntosh, who had grown up in the neighborhood, founded the school 10 years before, and built a haven for students of color in a city beset by racial discrimination and growing inequality. The school community was divided between those who saw the new principal as a symbol of gentrification and those who admired his eagerness to build on Brighter Choice's strengths and his commitment to fostering community.

The PTA had been in turmoil, as well. Some $7,000 had disappeared from the PTA bank account. The former PTA president, suspected of embezzlement, had left the school under a cloud. An atmosphere of mistrust prevailed. Parents who had raised money for the PTA through bake sales and donations felt betrayed.

If that wasn't bad enough, the children's scores on state reading and math tests had declined. In the spring of 2018, nearly half the children tested met state standards for math and reading. In the spring of 2019, Mr. Daniel's first year as principal, barely one third of the children passed the tests—well below the citywide rate of 46% for math and 47% for reading.

By June, a dozen parents (mostly White, a few Black) had withdrawn their children and enrolled them in charter schools or other schools outside the neighborhood—a worrisome sign of a lack of confidence in the school.

Still, September brings a fresh start and Keesha, who had been elected PTA president—unopposed—in June, was optimistic that this year would be better.

"It has the making of a very productive year," she told me over lunch at a coffee shop near the school later that day. "My goal this year is getting all the parents involved. My mission is to build bridges, close gaps. It gives us the opportunity to show the wonderful benefits of being together."

Keesha was filled with ideas to bring the community together: a family movie night, a Saturday trip to the carousel in Prospect Park. "We can learn how to speak to one another in a way that's not offensive," she said. "Ease the tensions." But she would confront mistrust, hurt feelings, and misunderstandings among different groups as they struggled to come to terms with dramatic demographic shifts in the neighborhood.

Brighter Choice, a neighborhood school that also accepts children from outside its attendance zone, is housed in a three-story red and beige brick building constructed in the 1960s. This part of Bedford-Stuyvesant has modest six-story apartment buildings, dollar stores, corner delis, and check-cashing businesses. The historic district of Stuyvesant Heights, with lush shade trees and $2 million Victorian brownstones, is a 15-minute walk to the south. A few blocks to the west are trendy bars and coffee shops—the beginning of neighborhood change. A few blocks to the north is a massive, 13-building public housing development called Sumner Houses; to the east are six more public housing towers that make up the Eleanor Roosevelt Houses.

For more than a century, Bedford-Stuyvesant has embodied both the high aspirations and deep disappointments of Black Americans in New York City. It has long been home to the Black elite, and even at a time when banks refused to give mortgages in the neighborhood, its gracious 19th-century brownstones offered the prospect of Black homeownership. Indeed, as early as the 1930s, immigrants from the West Indies who were excluded from conventional bank mortgages pooled their resources to create credit unions that provided loans at reasonable rates. (1)

In the years after World War II, Black migrants from the South seeking a better life crowded into Bedford-Stuyvesant, making it the largest Black community in New York City. The neighborhood was wracked by rising crime, underemployment, overcrowded schools, and inadequate municipal services. Yet it was also home to political activism, producing leaders of national prominence such as Rev. Milton Galamison, who led citywide protests against school segregation, and Shirley Chisholm, the nation's first Black congresswoman. It was the center of literary and musical expression, inspiring luminaries such as the poet June Jordan, the novelist Paule Marshall, the singer Lena Horne, the jazz drummer Max Roach, the filmmaker Spike Lee, and, more recently, the rappers Lil' Kim, Jay-Z, and Mos Def. (2)

Even during the neighborhood's most troubled years—through terrifying spikes in crime, waves of property abandonment, and the precipitous loss of population in the 1970s and 1980s, Bedford-Stuyvesant inspired loyalty among Black New Yorkers. It was a home with many problems, but it was a refuge from a larger city that seemed indifferent—or hostile—to Black aspirations. It was a place with a sense of community where neighbors said hello to one another, children jumped rope on the sidewalk, and families barbecued in local parks late into the night.

By 2019, Bedford-Stuyvesant was changing fast. Once predominantly Black, the community had become nearly 30% White. Housing costs were skyrocketing, and some long-time residents were being forced out. Gentrification didn't take over the whole neighborhood, however. A substantial core of low- and moderate-income people remained, protected from rapidly rising housing costs in the neighborhood's many rent-regulated apartments and public housing developments. In a country where the rich increasingly live in neighborhoods with other rich people and poor people live with other poor people, Bedford-Stuyvesant, where elegant brownstones abut public housing, is a place where rich and poor live next to one another. In a segregated city, Bedford-Stuyvesant is a place where children of different races and income levels could go to school together—at least in theory. However, theoretical possibilities and the reality on the ground are two different things.

Brighter Choice is located in District 16, one of the smallest of New York City's 32 school districts. Covering the eastern half of Bedford-Stuyvesant, District 16 is about a mile and a half from east to west and 2 miles north to south. For decades, District 16 schools have had a bad reputation—sometimes deserved, sometimes not—and they've been losing students at an alarming rate for years. While Bedford-Stuyvesant has become more racially and economically integrated in recent years, White

parents, as well as middle-class Black parents, tend to avoid the local schools, either because of prejudice or because of fears the schools have fewer resources and lower expectations for their pupils. Fully two thirds of the public school parents who live in District 16 take advantage of the city's extensive system of school choice to send their children to charter schools, gifted programs, or other schools outside the neighborhood. (3) On top of that, some families who live in District 16 send their children to private or religious schools—374 in 2019.

As parents with the most resources opt out, enrollments at traditional neighborhood schools collapse, leaving only the most vulnerable children. By 2019, 9 of the 13 elementary schools in the district had fewer than 300 children—in buildings designed to serve about 1,000 each. Four had fewer than 200 children and one, PS 25, had 74 children in prekindergarten through 5th grade in 2019—just 10 children in each grade. Schools with declining enrollments are caught in a downward spiral, with no easy way to recover.

District 16 has pockets of strength: PS 21 in the southern, more prosperous part of the district is a well-run and orderly school that even attracts children from outside the district. PS 40, near PS 21, has strong leadership and rising test scores and enrollment, even as other schools have seen their enrollments decline. Brooklyn Brownstone School, with an emphasis on character building, has a good attendance rate and above-average test scores.

Brighter Choice, with about 300 pupils, has a cheerful, well-kept building with a large playground and garden where children plant vegetables and learn about healthy food; the latest technology with electronic Smart Boards and plenty of laptops; and rich arts programming that includes African drumming and dance. Classes have fewer than 20 children—significantly less than the typical New York City class size of 25 to 30. The teaching staff is about half Black, one quarter Latino, and one quarter White, offering role models for children of different races. The warm and accessible new principal, Mr. Daniel, provides parents with his cell phone number so they can reach him easily.

Despite the turmoil of the previous year, the school had a solid core of parents who were willing to volunteer. Keesha's work as a customer service representative for Verizon had taught her to keep her cool when people got angry. Talia Braude, an architect and the PTA treasurer, and Lauren Harris, an occupational therapist and the PTA recording secretary, ably kept the books and took notes at meetings. Both White, they were carry-overs from the year before.

Five other parents had joined the PTA executive board since the scandal of the previous year. Four were African American women: the PTA vice president, Frances Toure, a billing specialist for a large law firm; Brandi Okesola, a lawyer; Shayla Coleman-Sutton, a speech therapist; and Ramona Dunlap, an actor and vocalist. The fifth, Jessica Hayden Mattheus, whose father is Irish American and whose mother is an immigrant from Peru, was the only Spanish-speaking member of the PTA executive board. Jessica, who runs a catering business, would serve as liaison to the school's Spanish-speaking parents.

Some staff members had their children at Brighter Choice, a sign of their confidence in the school. Kim Nunes, who is Black and who won a citywide "Blackboard Award" in recognition of her skill as a 5th-grade math teacher, sent her 1st-grade and 5th-grade daughters to the school. Deittra Wilder, whose son was in 1st grade, left a career as a lawyer to work as the "parent coordinator," or liaison to parents, at Brighter Choice. Ms. Deittra is African American, her husband is White, and theirs is one of the multiracial families at the school.

While most parent organizations are dominated by mothers, Brighter Choice also has active fathers. Ibrahim Toure, Frances's husband and a design engineer for New York City Transit, was part of a group called Fathers on a Mission, which was created to support fathers who wanted to be more involved with their children's lives. An at-home dad, Terrance Johnson, known as Coach TJ, is a frequent volunteer at the school. Most Saturdays, he's there to teach basketball.

Keesha took the reins of the PTA in the hopes that she could be involved in the day-to-day life of her son's school in the way that her own parents, because of their work schedules, could not be when she was a child. Having grown up in a working-class family a few miles from Bedford-Stuyvesant, she was also keenly aware of the struggles that low-income Black children face; she hoped her work as PTA president would ensure that these children remain included even as higher-income White families enrolled their children at Brighter Choice.

In 2013, Keesha moved to Bedford-Stuyvesant with her husband, Keyonn, who trains mentors for young people coming out of prison, and their baby son, also named Keyonn. When Little Keyonn was a toddler, they enrolled him at Little Sun People, a nursery school founded in 1980 by a long-time community activist, Fela Barclift, known as Mama Fela. Little Sun People is an Afrocentric school designed to insulate Black children from racism, build their self-confidence, and foster pride in their African American heritage.

At Little Sun People, children learn African dance and drumming. They sing African songs. All the teachers are Black, and children are taught that Black is beautiful. They learn about their world with field trips, such as going to a farm in Queens where they try their hands at milking a cow. Children are encouraged to speak up, and teachers listen and value what they have to say.

When the time came for elementary school, Keesha looked at private schools that promised individual attention, lots of class trips, and a curriculum based on exploration and play—some of the things that made Little Sun People attractive. But the private school price-tags were astronomical—more than $50,000 a year. Even if she had that kind of money, she was concerned that most private schools had staff and student bodies that were overwhelmingly White. Keesha didn't want her son to feel isolated as the only Black child in his class.

Brighter Choice offered a perfect alternative. Its founding principal, whom everyone called Ms. Fabayo, had attended Little Sun People herself as a child. Ms. Fabayo modeled Brighter Choice on Mama Fela's nursery school with its focus on Black culture and classrooms filled with joyful activities. Keesha enrolled Keyonn at Brighter Choice, assured that he would continue to have the self-confidence and pride in his African American heritage that Little Sun People had given him; she was hopeful that he would also learn about other peoples and cultures in their changing neighborhood.

For Keesha and her husband Keyonn, the changes in Bedford-Stuyvesant were a mixed bag. Over brunch one Saturday, they told me that some newcomers could be oblivious to the people who lived in the neighborhood before they arrived. As an example, Keyonn told me that someone complained to police one Sunday morning that the music from their church was too loud.

At the same time, Keyonn said, gentrification can be an opportunity to get more resources to their neighborhood and their school. Some White parents, with expectations based on their own experiences at well-resourced schools, make demands of the school system that can help all children. At

Brighter Choice, for example, a White father applied for and received a grant to build a science lab.

"Parents before just believed that we had to go with whatever was given," Keyonn said. "New parents are coming in, they are like, 'Hey, I don't just have to put up with that. How come we don't have this? Well, why can't we have that? We should have more.'"

Like it or not, gentrification is a reality, Keyonn said, and it's best to take advantage of its possible benefits while trying to limit its ill-effects. "Now we are together," Keesha added. "If we deal with it, we can change the dynamic. Let's be the school that ignites change citywide."

Keesha's work as PTA president would be a tricky balancing act. She wanted Brighter Choice to continue to be a place where African American children felt safe, and where their identity was validated. At the same time, she wanted to open the doors to all in the neighborhood.

Keesha would serve as PTA president for the next 3 years, a time that would test whether the school's strengths would be enough to overcome its many challenges: low test scores, high rates of absenteeism, the lack of air-conditioning, an atmosphere of mistrust within the PTA, and bad feelings about the district's hiring of a White principal in a majority Black school. The COVID-19 pandemic—which would kill tens of thousands of New Yorkers, severely disrupt public education, and deepen the divide between the city's haves and have-nots—would only add to these challenges.

Keesha's tenure as PTA president would test whether Brighter Choice could avoid the fate of other District 16 schools whose shrinking enrollments left them with declining budgets, growing proportions of the city's most vulnerable children, and no clear path forward. Brighter Choice was up against decades of disinvestment in Black neighborhoods, housing discrimination, and failed efforts at school reform that have divided neighborhoods, schools, and families. But Brighter Choice also had a strength to build on: the legacy of community activists committed to educating Black children against tremendous odds. One of these activists is Mama Fela, whose life experiences reveal both the deep roots of inequality in the city's school system and the possibilities for Black children to have access to equal opportunity.

TWO

The Roots of Inequality and the Struggle for Just Schools

courtesy of Little Sun People

For Mama Fela, all-Black schools are a refuge in a hostile world.

Little Sun People, Mama Fela's nursery school and child care center, is housed in a few small rooms, some without windows, in a former office building in Bedford-Stuyvesant. But the modest space is richly equipped with places for children to learn and explore: bookshelves stuffed with wooden blocks and DUPLO® bricks, tables where children can paint or mold clay, a corner where they learn African dance or sing Gospel and jazz tunes, another where they learn to cook African recipes. The grown-ups—called "Mama" and their first name, in an African custom—speak to them gently and with respect.

Little Sun People has been a community institution for decades, giving generations of children in Bedford-Stuyvesant pride in their African American heritage and the confidence and curiosity they need to succeed in school. Mama Fela founded Little Sun People in 1980 for her own children, hoping to protect them from the racism that she and her siblings endured in public schools in Brooklyn in the 1950s and 1960s. Mama Fela's childhood—during the struggles of the Civil Rights movement and the violent White backlash against even modest plans to integrate schools—taught her that an all-Black school with all-Black teachers, like Little Sun People, could be a refuge from a hostile world. Her experiences help explain why some Black parents today see Black empowerment—not integration—as the best way to ensure their children have access to equal educational opportunities.

Born in Georgia in 1949, Mama Fela moved to New York City with her mother, who was then pregnant with her sister; her father; and her baby brother in 1951. They were part of the second wave of the Great Migration of African Americans to the North, escaping extreme poverty and the Jim Crow laws that enforced segregation in the South.

Her parents had been sharecroppers, part of the system of tenant farming in which families rented a plot of land from a White landlord, paying him a portion or "share" of their crops.

"At the end of the year when it was time to share up, [my mother's] parents would always come home with nothing," Mama Fela told me. "After working a whole year picking cotton and picking whatever it was that they were growing there, they didn't have anything at all. And my dad's family, the same thing."

Her father had been a U.S. Army cook stationed in Paris in World War II, where he got a glimpse of what life could be like free of discrimination. "There was so much deference they had to have in the South," Mama Fela said. "You couldn't even ask for an opportunity. You had to keep your head down and do what you were told. And they heard these stories about how you could come to the North and be free and have an opportunity to make it and make a good living and have a good life for yourself and your family and you could hold your head up. That's what they wanted," she said.

Her family settled in Bedford-Stuyvesant, and her father got what seemed like a good job at a carpet factory in Brooklyn, earning enough money that her mother could stay home with the children. When her family arrived, they were the only Black family on their block. But within a year of arriving in Bedford-Stuyvesant, she said, all the White people moved out.

Brooklyn, like other Northern urban areas, underwent a profound demographic transformation after World War II as Black and Puerto Rican migrants moved in and White residents moved to the newly built suburbs or clustered in a few predominantly White Brooklyn neighborhoods.

This dramatic change didn't happen by chance. As Richard Rothstein argues in *The Color of Law*, federal housing policy, beginning in the 1930s and continuing through the 1960s, created all-Black urban neighborhoods and all-White suburbs, starving the cities of investment while pouring resources into the suburbs. The federal government, as part of the New Deal, subsidized and guaranteed mortgages to expand home ownership and prevent foreclosures. But rather than giving mortgages to all qualified borrowers, federal agencies conducted appraisals to determine which neighborhoods were considered "safe" for investment and which were "risky."

The Federal Housing Authority refused to guarantee mortgages in neighborhoods with even a small percentage of Black residents (as well as those with a high proportion of foreign-born Jewish or Italian residents). This policy was known as redlining. Bedford-Stuyvesant was mostly White in the 1930s (the few Black households included middle-class homeowners), but the federal government, as well as the banks, deemed it too risky for investment. (1)

As Black families like Mama Fela's moved to Bedford-Stuyvesant after World War II, banks refused loans even though foreclosure rates were lower than in other neighborhoods. Redlining was a self-fulfilling prophecy. Homeowners had trouble getting loans for maintenance and repairs. Properties deteriorated and values declined. White homeowners in redlined neighborhoods could watch their investments decline, or sell and move to neighborhoods where the government would guarantee mortgages. Blockbusting real estate agents stoked fears to encourage White homeowners to sell at low prices, then resold to Black buyers for a profit. (2)

The impact of redlining would be felt for years to come. For example, decades later, redlined neighborhoods would have fewer trees, more concrete and higher temperatures. Hotter neighborhoods were associated with lower test scores among children, particularly in schools without air-conditioning. Redlining is also associated with poor health: During the coronavirus pandemic in 2020, the rate of infections for COVID-19 would be higher in neighborhoods that had been redlined. (3)

For White Brooklynites in the years after World War II, the new suburbs beckoned. They could get government-subsidized mortgages with low interest rates and no down payment. But Black households had few alternatives to redlined neighborhoods. Suburban developers, partly out of their own prejudices, partly to maintain their access to government-subsidized mortgages, barred sales to Black buyers. For example, Levittown, the massive Long Island development of modest single-family houses constructed after World War II, included racial covenants in its deeds, even after the Supreme Court declared them unenforceable in 1948. In the original leases, Black people were prohibited even as guests. (4)

In Brooklyn and across the nation, real estate agents routinely refused to sell or rent to Black tenants in White neighborhoods. Even John Hope Franklin, the distinguished African American historian, could not find housing near Brooklyn College when he was hired as head of the all-White history department in 1957. Black Americans who tried to live in White neighborhoods faced violence: When a Black mother, Irene Willins, moved her family from Bedford-Stuyvesant to an Italian American neighborhood called South Brooklyn (now Cobble Hill) in 1960, someone threw rocks through her windows and set fire to piles of debris in a vacant lot next door. In every borough, there were firebombings, cross burnings, and other violent terrorist acts. (5)

Black families like Mama Fela's arriving from the South crowded into Bedford-Stuyvesant, making it one of the largest African American communities in the country. As the population swelled, houses were divided into small apartments and families doubled and tripled up. As buildings decayed and rents skyrocketed, city services deteriorated. For example, even as Bedford-Stuyvesant's population quadrupled from the 1940s to the 1960s, the sanitation department continued to pick up garbage just three times a week. Garbage piled up on the streets. In a 1962 protest, the Congress of Racial Equality, an interracial group, picked up all the garbage the sanitation men left on the street and dumped it at Brooklyn Borough Hall. (6)

As a child, Mama Fela may not have known this history. But she certainly remembers the impact it had on her family. By the time Mama Fela, known as Frances at the time, started school, overcrowding was endemic because school construction failed to keep pace with the burgeoning population. Some children in Bedford-Stuyvesant had just 4 hours of instruction so that schools could accommodate two shifts: one in the morning and one in the afternoon. (7)

The teachers' union insisted that staffers with the most seniority be given their choice of assignments; those with the least experience wound up at Black schools. The city had so much trouble staffing schools, particularly in Black neighborhoods, that it would hire people with little training or qualifications. Books and supplies were scarce. Mama Fela's classmates reacted to the terrible conditions by lashing out. "The kids were always fighting," Mama Fela recalled. "People turned in all the anger on themselves."

Her parents moved to the adjacent neighborhood, Crown Heights, hoping for better schools. But her junior high school, JHS 210, was even worse. "That was one of the most scary experiences in my life," she recalled. "I don't know how I got out of there alive. I would hide out in the bathroom and wait until practically everyone was gone. And then I would sneak out, race home as fast as I could get there."

Newspapers at the time were writing about crime waves in the schools; a reporter for the World Telegram, George Allen, wrote a book called *Undercover Teacher* in which he recounted how a blind 13-year-old girl was raped in the stairwell of JHS 210 in 1958, 2 years before Mama Fela enrolled. In hyperbolic prose, Allen said: "Teenage mobs literally ruled some schools. Frightened parents made plans to move out of the city. Teachers resigned or simply never showed up for their job." (8)

Allen, who worked as a teacher for just 2 months in 1958 to gather material for his expose, said teachers referred to JHS 210 as a "jungle," called the students "animals," and boasted that they "smacked [the students] around" when no one was looking. A rigid tracking system effectively abandoned all but the most advanced students. Children were given IQ tests to determine what track they should be in. Perhaps not surprisingly, the longer they stayed in school, the more their IQs declined. Those with IQs below 85 were not allowed to take remedial reading classes, which were reserved for children deemed to have more promise.

Tracking sometimes sorted children to an absurd degree. Clarence Taylor, who would go on to become a distinguished African American historian at the City University of New York, was relegated to a track near the bottom—19th out of 23—at his gigantic junior high school in East New York, not far from Bedford-Stuyvesant. (9)

As Mama Fela remembers it, there were a few White students in her classes when she began 7th grade in 1960; there were none by the time she graduated 3 years later. All her teachers were White; the curriculum excluded any reference to the African American experience. Her social studies history book had just one page on slavery, she recalled, with a picture that suggested bondage wasn't so bad. "Slaves were dancing and smiling, and they looked really happy," she said.

Meanwhile, things took a turn for the worse at home. Her father was a good worker who expected to be promoted and get raises. But racial discrimination kept him in a low-level job. "He hit a ceiling pretty fast. He became bitter. His dreams were dashed," she said. She blames his deep disappointment on what happened next.

"He turned in on his anger. He ended up losing his mind. He ended up in a mental hospital." He was never the same afterwards, although he came home to live. Her mother went to work in a hospital kitchen and took over running the household. Her family, like millions of others, had moved North in search of well-paid manufacturing jobs. But those jobs were disappearing in the 1960s. The Brooklyn Navy Yard, which built battleships in World War II and the Korean War, closed in 1966; sugar refineries and breweries closed as well. (10)

"There was hopelessness and despair—all those people who came out of enslavement and Jim Crow, going to the North with all these hopes and dreams and finding the hopes and dreams to be nothing but bitter ashes," Mama Fela said. "You don't know what to do with yourself. And so that anger. You just lash out."

While Mama Fela was in junior high school, Black civil rights leaders in Brooklyn were fighting for school desegregation—not as an end in itself, but as a way to ensure that Black children had access to the same resources as White children.

"Negroes don't need segregated or integrated schools in themselves," said the Rev. Milton Galamison, who organized a massive boycott on Feb. 3, 1964, demanding desegregation of New York City's public schools. "What Negroes do need is an equal education and it happens this is impossible in a segregated school."

The Board of Education calculated that 464,362 pupils joined the protest, about 45% of the total enrollment of 1,037,757; the civil rights leader Bayard Rustin, one of the organizers, estimated one fifth of the boycotters were White. For a brief time, Black, Puerto Rican, and some White New Yorkers came together to demand integrated schools. (11)

But, as historian Peter Eisenstadt has noted, support for integration was "wide but shallow and lukewarm" while opposition was "heated and vociferous." Even small-scale attempts at integration—whether busing Black children into White schools or "pairing" Black and White schools in adjacent neighborhoods—were met with organized, vicious opposition from White parents. (12)

For Mama Fela, integration didn't seem to solve anything. In fact, it sometimes made things worse. When she enrolled at Wingate High School in 1964, the school was "integrated," but Black and White students were mostly segregated within the building. Mama Fela was one of a tiny number of Black students assigned to the "academic" or college prep track, on the top floor. On the second floor was the commercial track, vocational training for secretarial work. "Nothing but Black girls, all typing away," she recalled. The general track was on the ground floor, which she passed through only once. "Nothing but Black boys. They were either playing dice, or asleep, or playing games. The teacher was a White man with his feet on the desk, reading *The New York Times*. I couldn't believe it. It was a nightmare." She recalled one White teacher would walk past her and literally flinch. "Like she hated me. And it wasn't anything I had done. It wasn't personal. It was just racism."

As bad as school was for her, it was worse for her younger brother and sister, who were part of the Board of Education's modest plan to send Black and Puerto Rican children from overcrowded schools to White schools that had empty seats. While Mama Fela was assigned to schools not far from home, her brother and sister were bused to Bensonhurst, an all-White neighborhood 5 miles away. Mama Fela recalls how White crowds—adults as well as children—used to gather round the buses to jeer at the Black children when they arrived.

"People spit on them and cursed them. They called them the 'N' word. They threw things at the bus, bottles and cans. Busing was a nightmare for them," Mama Fela said. "I just missed busing by a thread and I'm so glad."

Her own parents couldn't do much to help. Her father was disabled with mental illness and her mother, who had very limited education in a one-room schoolhouse in Georgia, didn't know how to fight the bureaucracy. "She did not know how to advocate for us," Mama Fela said. "She would only know how to follow directions."

The White backlash to busing was politically potent. One month after Galamison's giant school boycott, more than 10,000 White mothers who called themselves Parents and Taxpayers (PAT) marched in the snow across the Brooklyn Bridge to City Hall to protest plans to bus Black children to White schools. Six months later, PAT organized a boycott of their own: More than 275,000 children stayed home on Sept 14, 1964.

In Washington, lawmakers responded to the White anger over busing by defending the type of school segregation that was prevalent in the North—that is, "de facto" segregation caused by housing segregation—while attacking the "de jure" segregation that was prevalent in the South—that is, two legally separate school systems, one for Black students, one for White students.

The Civil Rights Act of 1964 outlawed racial discrimination in housing, employment, and education, and authorized the federal government to desegregate schools. But Northern lawmakers inserted a clause that historian Matthew Delmont calls "the anti-busing loophole." The clause, section 401 of Title IV, stipulates that "'desegregation' shall not mean the assignment of students to public schools in order to overcome racial imbalance." In short, so-called "de jure" segregation was banned, but nothing would be done about "de facto" segregation. While a few individual schools in New York City would come under court-ordered desegregation plans, there would be no citywide desegregation order. The anti-busing loophole is one reason why New York's schools today are more segregated than many school systems in the South. (13)

By the end of the 1960s, the city had all but abandoned its attempts, however limited, at desegregation. Even if there had been a political will for it, large-scale integration was no longer feasible because so many White families had moved to the suburbs. Many Black and Puerto Rican community activists and their White allies came to believe that community control of schools—not integration—held the most promise for high-quality education for their children. Community control, these activists believed, would lead to increased hiring of Black and Puerto Rican principals, teachers, and school aides to teach Black and Puerto Rican children as well as a curriculum more attuned to their history and culture.

Community control was also an attractive idea for the city's political leadership. New York City had largely escaped the race riots that wracked many U.S. cities in the summer of 1967, and Mayor John Lindsay, elected in 1965, believed community control could help keep the temperature in New York down. "By going along with community control, Lindsay could be seen as helping to head off a Black revolution without having to demand anything from angry White parents," said Mark Winston Griffith, executive director of the Brooklyn Movement Center, a community organization in Bedford-Stuyvesant. (14)

In 1967, with support from the Ford Foundation, the city launched an experiment in community control in three "demonstration districts": East Harlem, the Lower East Side in Manhattan, and Ocean Hill–Brownsville in Brooklyn, a neighborhood adjacent to Bedford-Stuyvesant. The central Board of Education authorized residents in these districts to elect their own school-governing boards that would appoint principals, set standards, and decide on curriculum. Responding to parents' complaints, the new boards eliminated tracking, introduced African American history, and taught Swahili in some schools. In Ocean Hill–Brownsville, the board appointed a Black superintendent, Rhody McCoy, and hired five Black principals. (15)

From the start, there was friction between proponents of community control and the teachers' union. The bad blood burst into an open conflict in 1968 when McCoy removed 13 teachers and six administrators, all White, from Junior High School 271 in Ocean Hill–Brownsville in what the union said was a violation of the teachers' contract. The United Federation of Teachers called a citywide strike that lasted 7 weeks.

The strike pitted a mostly White teachers' union against Black and Puerto Rican parents who wanted the power to hire people they felt shared their aspirations for their children. It deepened racial divisions, ending the possibility of an interracial alliance to improve schools that had seemed possible, however briefly, during Galamison's huge boycott in 1964. (16)

The strike led to compromise legislation that gave proponents of community control only a small portion of the power which they had sought. The State Legislature gave control of elementary and junior high schools to 31 (later 32) locally elected community school districts—districts whose boundaries continue to this day. These boards could draw lines for school attendance zones, appoint superintendents, hire principals, and set education policy for each community. The high schools, however, remained under the jurisdiction of the central Board of Education, and the teachers' contract was bargained centrally—dashing the hopes of community control activists.

In 1969, when the jagged district lines were drawn, there was still some potential for integration within the city's five boroughs. The state legislature, facing competing demands, drew districts that exacerbated

District lines from 1969 contribute to inequality today.

segregation in some neighborhoods and left open the possibility of integration in others.

District 2, for example, snaked across Manhattan, bringing together far-apart White neighborhoods like the Upper East Side and Greenwich Village, leaving out adjacent Puerto Rican neighborhoods like the Lower East Side and East Harlem.

In Brooklyn, District 16, a mostly Black neighborhood in the Eastern part of Bedford-Stuyvesant, was split off from District 32 in neighboring Bushwick, which was White at the time of decentralization. District 20 encompassed the then-White neighborhoods of Bay Ridge, Bensonhurst, and Dyker Heights.

Several Brooklyn districts were drawn to include White, Black, and Puerto Rican neighborhoods. Two of these, District 13 and District 15, have the most integrated schools today. District 13 includes the stately homes of Brooklyn Heights and a mix of brownstones and public housing projects in Fort Greene, Clinton Hill, and the western part of Bedford-Stuyvesant. District 15 includes the townhouses of Park Slope, the immigrant communities of Sunset Park, and the industrial waterfront of Red Hook.

The district lines, more than half a century old, are at the root of much of the inequality in New York City schools today. In more affluent and White districts, it's easier to recruit and retain superintendents, principals, and staff. In addition, parents may raise money for the PTA and offer their children tutoring and enrichment outside of class. It's true that the city's low-income districts, serving mostly Black and Latino children, receive more federal aid and spend more per pupil than the high-income districts serving mostly White and Asian children. (17) But the slight advantage in funding is offset by the other challenges faced by high-poverty schools.

Any inequalities among districts in New York City, however, are dwarfed by the inequality between the city and wealthy suburban districts. That's because of our country's tradition of localism. In the United States, each city or town is charged with operating its own school system, paid for primarily with local property taxes—unlike countries with a national commitment to educational equity. Rich towns can tax themselves at a low rate and raise lots of money, while poor towns must tax themselves at a high rate to have even mediocre schools. State and federal money offsets some of these gaps. Still, as a *New York Times* editorial points out, "The United States is virtually alone among developed nations in devoting more public resources to educating affluent children than poor children." (18)

The resulting inequality has the blessing of the U.S. Supreme Court. While the Supreme Court outlawed school segregation in its famous 1954 decision, two less well-known cases in the 1970s affirmed the legitimacy of unequal funding across district lines and undermined the promise of *Brown v. Board of Education*. In one case, Mexican American parents in San Antonio, Texas, challenged the funding scheme that left their district with far less money than a wealthy White one nearby. In the 1973 decision, *San Antonio Independent School District v. Rodriguez*, the court upheld the unequal funding, saying education is not a right enumerated in the Constitution.

The following year, in *Milliken v. Bradley*, the court overturned a plan that would have bused Black students from Detroit to schools in all-White suburbs. President Richard Nixon had appointed four justices, and the court had shifted its philosophy since *Brown v. Board*. Thurgood Marshall, who had argued *Brown* for the NAACP and had been appointed to the Supreme Court in 1967, said the *Milliken* decision was a "giant step backwards," and, in his dissent, called district lines "fences to separate the races."

Decentralization came too late to affect Mama Fela's school experiences. After graduating from Wingate High School in 1967, she enrolled in Brooklyn College under a special program designed to help high-achieving Black students from low-income families. She joined the Black Power movement and taught at an Afrocentric school. She eventually graduated from college and went on to receive a masters' degree from Bank Street College of Education in Manhattan, which has a national reputation for training teachers who foster small children's curiosity and independent thinking. But she said her brother and sister never recovered from the trauma of being bused to a hostile White neighborhood. They both dropped out of school. Her brother died of AIDS in 1986. Her sister is disabled and lives in a nursing home.

At the end of my visit to Little Sun People and the interview with Mama Fela, I told her about Keesha's mission to bring together families of different races at Brighter Choice. Mama Fela frowned and shook her head.

"I don't know," she replied. "It's two different camps there. I just don't see them being able to come together. Most of the Black kids will probably leave and the ones who stay will become very assimilated and it will become a mostly White school."

She paused, and then went on.

"I do believe integration could potentially work someday. But until we have the conversations about race and racism that we need to have, it's not going to work. There is too much bitterness and anger. White people don't want to talk about it? We'll let it go. We won't talk about it. But that doesn't really help with the understanding that needs to happen if integration is ever going to work."

THREE

The Deep Decline and Uneven Revival of the City's Schools

courtesy of John Dewey High School Archives

Keesha's high school yearbook: An integrated oasis. Keesha, bottom right.

Keesha had an easier time in school—and better experiences at an integrated high school—than Mama Fela and her siblings did. That may be why she's more optimistic that people of different races can learn to get along at Brighter Choice. Her school experiences were a mixed bag, but, nonetheless, they left her hopeful about the possibilities for a good education for her son.

Keesha came of age in the 1970s and 1980s, a time of urban strife and dramatic demographic changes in the city. The way the city responded to these challenges helps explain the deep inequality in the school system today.

In the 1960s, Keesha's parents moved to Brooklyn from McClellanville and Beaufort, South Carolina, part of the ongoing Great Migration of African Americans from the South. Her father was a printer and a pastor. Her mother was a preschool teacher.

Born in 1973, Keesha attended elementary and junior high school in the years after the 1975 fiscal crisis, when the city's schools, hit by drastic budget cuts, were in a sad state and rising crime and disorder seemed to doom the city. In the late 1970s and early 1980s, Keesha attended PS 273, just a block from her home in the Boulevard Houses public housing development in East New York, a few miles from Bedford-Stuyvesant. PS 273 had nearly 1,000 students, mostly Black, with about 150 Latino children and a handful of White children. Keesha remembers school plays, spelling bees, storytelling contests, and music lessons. The school had a warm sense of community, and, when the children sang Christmas songs at an evening concert, a large number of neighborhood residents showed up to listen and show their support. Before Keesha graduated, an African American woman was named principal. Keesha was in a "gifted" class with other bright children.

It wasn't a perfect school. The textbooks were worn and out-of-date, and the teachers, who thought children should be seen and not heard, tended to stand and talk from the front of the room rather than encourage class discussions. The teachers were mostly White, and the curriculum hardly mentioned African Americans or their contributions to the nation. The public library helped make up for what was missing at school.

"Growing up in the 'hood, my parents took me to the library to see books with people who looked like me," Keesha said. "I didn't see that in the schools. They taught me, 'This is who you are, this is where you come from, this is where you can go.'"

Her junior high school, JHS 166, George Gershwin, was one of the lowest performing, most unruly schools in the city. It had a rigid tracking system, and children in the bottom tracks would take out their resentment on kids in the higher tracks. Children would pick fights with Keesha, who was in the gifted track, and taunt her with "You think you're smart?"

"Did I get into fights?" she said. "Yes, I did. I knew friends whose parents pulled them from public schools and put them in Catholic schools. I'm sure there were schools in other areas that had more and better, but it was all I knew so I didn't have much to compare it to."

While her elementary school experience had been good and junior high had been tolerable, her zoned neighborhood high school, Thomas Jefferson High School, was a violent place where few students stayed around to graduate.

Keesha's older cousin, whom she idolized, had attended an alternative school called John Dewey High School in Gravesend, a mostly White neighborhood about 8 miles from East New York. Keesha's Sunday School teacher, Frances Hagler, who also worked for the Board of Education, helped guide Keesha through the application process for Dewey. She was accepted and enrolled in 1988. The school was in the neighborhood adjacent to Bensonhurst, where Mama Fela's brother and sister had been bused.

It was a grueling commute. The city allowed children to attend schools outside their neighborhood, space permitting, but high school students were not eligible for transportation by yellow school bus. The subway connections were poor, and city buses were slow and unreliable. Keesha remembers getting up at 4:30 A.M. each morning to leave the house by 5:45 A.M. It was a 2-hour commute, and classes started at 8 A.M.

The long ride was worth it, however. When Keesha arrived at school each day, she found an environment that was much calmer than her junior high school had been. John Dewey High School, founded in 1969, was designed to bring together students from different neighborhoods and with different academic abilities. Based on the progressive philosophy of its namesake, it was the first "educational option" school in New York City, with an admissions formula that enrolled fixed ratios of students with high-, average- and below-average test scores.

"It looked like a college campus, and there were students from everywhere. It was my first experience with people of other races—Asian, Caucasian, Indian. There were hippie kids, heavy metal kids. It was eclectic," Keesha said. "There was more there, the books, the teaching. Although it was a high school, it operated more like a college." Instead of English 9, students could choose courses like "Detective Stories and Mysteries" or "The

Bible as Literature." "Dewey was great for me. It gave me a perspective that I didn't have before. I was exposed to so much."

For Keesha, Dewey was liberating, challenging, and fun, its own little melting pot with students of different races and cultures drawn from across Brooklyn. But it was an oasis in a troubled system.

The 1970s and 1980s were a dire time for New York City and its schools, not just in poor neighborhoods but in middle-class neighborhoods as well. Industrial jobs were leaving the city; unemployment and crime were rising. The city's population and its tax revenues shrank in the 1970s and, by 1975, the city could no longer pay its bills and nearly went bankrupt. When the federal government and President Gerald Ford refused help, *The Daily News* captured the city's distress in the famous headline: "Ford to City: Drop Dead." If the austerity that followed was presented as a kind of cure for the city's insolvency, it was a cure that was worse than the disease.

School budgets were decimated. The city laid off 11,000 teachers, or one fifth of the workforce, as well as 10,000 classroom aides (called paraprofessionals) and other school employees. The school week was shortened by 90 minutes, class sizes grew, sports and after-school programs were eliminated, and school-based dental and medical clinics closed. Art and music teachers, guidance counselors, and school librarians were let go. Buildings deteriorated as maintenance was deferred.

"They have cut out everything that makes school enjoyable," an elementary school teacher in Bedford-Stuyvesant told *The New York Times* in 1976. The layoffs hurt Black and Puerto Rican staffers particularly hard: Young teachers and paraprofessionals, who were more likely to be Black or Puerto Rican, were laid off first because they had the least seniority. The layoffs came in waves throughout the 1975–1976 school year, so class assignments were repeatedly juggled as junior teachers were removed and replaced by more senior teachers. Some classrooms had eight different teachers in a year.

Truancy increased after attendance teachers were laid off; one department store complained of children hanging out during school hours. "The main thing a lot of kids seem to be learning is shoplifting," a school official told the *Times*. A school superintendent who lost half his guidance counselors said there was a long list of children waiting for psychological services—bringing havoc to many classrooms. "One disruptive child can prevent the education of 29 others," this official said. (1)

The city lost 10% of its population in the 1970s. School enrollment dropped from 1.1 million in 1978 to 924,000 in 1982, an even steeper decline than the decrease in the city's population overall. The school budget declined 25% in constant dollars from 1975 to 1980. All major urban school systems in the United States made budget cuts, but New York City's was among the most drastic. (2)

The city's schools were in a downward spiral, with no obvious way to recover. Even parents of modest means—both White and Black—avoided them, enrolling their children in private or parochial schools. The proportion of poor children in the city schools grew—and it was a different kind of poverty, with increasing numbers of families relying on welfare. "The difference between poor and dependent poor," said Deputy School Chancellor Bernard R. Gifford, who himself grew up on welfare in Bedford-Stuyvesant, "is the difference between a father who does not make enough to get his income above the poverty level and a situation where the father does not work at all." (3)

Combined with savage budget cuts, these demographic changes made it even harder for the city's schools to succeed. The sad fact is that the turmoil of the 1960s combined with the fiscal crisis of the 1970s led the middle class to abandon the public schools—and that spelled trouble for decades to come.

The middle-class exodus was particularly pronounced in Bedford-Stuyvesant. The neighborhood's population declined by 30% from 1970 to 1980; the number of children under the age of 18 dropped by half. This decline was partly the result of the 1968 Fair Housing Act which outlawed racial discrimination. With more choices in housing, some Black families left for the suburbs; others moved to Black middle-class enclaves in New York City such as St. Albans, Queens. As the sociologist William Julius Wilson argues, the exodus of middle- and working-class Black households left many inner-city neighborhoods with high concentrations of poverty, high levels of unemployment, and more people he calls "the truly disadvantaged." (4) While the Black elite never completely abandoned Bedford-Stuyvesant's stately Victorian townhouses and tree-lined streets, the neighborhood—and its schools—suffered.

Into the late 1980s, the city's schools were in a sorry state, not just in Black and Puerto Rican neighborhoods, but in White ones as well. It was a grim sort of equality: All the public schools struggled. New teachers would routinely wait 2 months for their first paycheck because of a glitch in the city's payroll system. Students sat on windowsills or radiator covers because there weren't enough desks. Elementary school students had classes in old bathrooms or closets. Even Bronx High School of Science, one of the city's most celebrated schools, was not spared the dismal conditions: More than 300 shattered windows were not repaired for months because of a dispute with the custodians' union. No one at the top of city government seemed to be invested in the public schools. In 1987, not one member of the Board of Education and not one citywide elected official had a child in public school. Turnover at the top was rapid. In the 1980s, the city had five school chancellors. (5)

Crime gripped the city and violence overflowed into the schools as well. At the most troubled high schools, some students carried guns and knives to class. There were reports of stabbings and even shootings. In January 1988, officials had to stop an inspection of Park West High School in Manhattan and leave because conditions were so "chaotic." A low point came in 1992 at Thomas Jefferson High School—the school Keesha had avoided by going to Dewey. Just minutes before Mayor David Dinkins arrived for a visit, two students were shot dead. (6)

But even as crime and mismanagement overwhelmed the schools, a new force was reshaping the city, reversing the population declines of the 1970s and revitalizing some neighborhoods and schools: immigration. If the fiscal crisis of the 1970s devastated all schools, the city's response to demographic changes in the 1980s led to an uneven revival: In some neighborhoods, schools flourished. In others, schools continued to struggle. The role of immigrants, particularly Chinese immigrants, helps explain at least a part of the thorny question of why neighborhoods just a few miles apart from one another have schools that vary so much in quality.

Under a 1924 law, immigration to the United States had been mostly limited to people from northern Europe. That changed when the Immigration and Naturalization Act of 1965, inspired by civil rights legislation, opened the doors to people from a broad range of countries. The new law favored relatives of U.S. citizens and, to a lesser extent, people with special skills.

A trickle of Chinese immigrants grew to a flood after 1976 when Chairman Deng Xiaoping opened the country to emigration. Political instability and economic woes triggered migration from Central America, the West Indies, Haiti, and the Dominican Republic.

By 1982, the city had more than 1 million immigrants. By 2010, there were more than 3 million, making up 37% of the city's population. Immigrants and their U.S.-born children together made up 55% of the city's population. Newcomers restored neighborhoods, fixing up abandoned houses and opening small businesses in vacant storefronts. With more people around, neighborhoods became safer.

In Brooklyn, Chinese immigrants opened grocery stores, beauty salons, restaurants, and outlets for herbal medicine along 8th Avenue in Sunset Park, a neighborhood that would become one of the biggest Chinatowns in the city. West Indian immigrants opened record stores, tropical fruit stands, and bakeries on Fulton Street and Nostrand Avenue in Bedford-Stuyvesant, filling the air with the sounds of reggae and calypso and the aromas of mangoes and coconut bread, as the writer Paule Marshall recalled in 1985. (7) Immigrants from the Dominican Republic and Mexico settled across Brooklyn. Keesha recalls that the vitality of her high school came from the range of students who enrolled, including immigrants from the West Indies and Asia.

School enrollments boomed in immigrant neighborhoods, particularly in areas where Chinese families settled. As many White and Black middle-class families avoided the public schools, Chinese immigrant families, with little money or knowledge about private schools, saw no alternative to public schooling. Some Chinese immigrants had high levels of education and were able to offer their children the support they needed to be successful in school, even if their incomes were low.

For example, Sherry Yan, who had been a middle-school teacher in her native China, and her husband, who had been a college professor in China, came to New York City in the late 1980s on student visas to continue their education. They moved to Bensonhurst, the Italian American neighborhood where hostile crowds had attacked school buses carrying Mama Fela's brother and sister in the 1960s.

Hostility toward Black people continued well into the 1980s. In 1989, Yusef Hawkins, a Black teenager from Bedford-Stuyvesant, went to Bensonhurst to buy a used car and was chased by a White mob and shot dead. The following week, hundreds of angry White residents lined the streets of Bensonhurst and shouted racial slurs at marchers who protested the murder.

If Black people were not welcome in Bensonhurst, Asian and Latino people were at least tolerated. Long-time residents mostly ignored the newcomers from China, Sherry told me. "It was not too bad. Just okay," Sherry recalled when I met her in early 2020. "They don't talk to us, but they don't do something bad to us."

Sherry enrolled her daughter Lulu at PS 127 in District 20, which serves Bensonhurst, Dyker Heights, and Bay Ridge. Some children made fun of Lulu because she didn't speak English. A little boy once locked her in the bathroom just to tease her, a frightening experience that made her cry. But the girl picked up English quickly and, overall, did well in school.

Sherry and her husband were approved for permanent residency, or green cards, because the Board of Education desperately needed bilingual teachers for the wave of new immigrants. They both got jobs in junior high schools.

At times, the work was discouraging. Schools were still recovering from the fiscal crisis of 1975, and teachers faced poor pay, large classes, and some angry and alienated students. Sherry's husband, who had taught at the university level in China, was used to the respect customarily given to teachers in his home country. At the junior high school where he taught, unruly students frustrated him so much that he considered quitting. But his chance for permanent residency in the United States depended on the teaching job, so he persevered.

Little by little, the elementary and middle schools in Brooklyn's District 20 got better. In 1994, the local school board appointed an effective superintendent, Vincent Grippo, who improved the quality of teacher training, added arts programming (including Suzuki violin classes and a partnership with the Metropolitan Opera), and strengthened services in special education and English as a Second Language. (8) New pupils included the children of highly educated immigrants from the former Soviet Union and China—families who had high expectations for their children's education but who were too poor to consider private schools. District 20 was in a virtuous cycle: As the schools' reputation improved, parents increasingly moved to the district to enroll their children. Between 1983 and 2018, elementary school enrollments doubled. And, because budgets are pegged to enrollments, school budgets increased as well. While the schools continued to serve large numbers of low-income children, the mix of children from different family incomes (and education levels) was critical to the district's success.

Sherry would create what one District 20 parent leader, Stanley Ng, calls the district's "secret sauce" for student success. In the late 1990s, Sherry opened a center called A+ Academy with after-school, Saturday, and summer classes to help children prepare for the competitive exam to the specialized high schools. Other test prep centers opened as well, serving many Asian immigrants. The supplemental education offered by these centers—where tuition was a fraction of that of even moderately priced parochial schools—not only helped children gain access to the specialized high schools, it also boosted their skills in elementary and middle school, making it easier for their neighborhood schools to succeed.

Asian immigrants may have helped revive schools in a few neighborhoods in the late 1980s and early 1990s, but most of the city's public schools still had a terrible reputation. That, too, began to change, haltingly and unevenly, as the result of another demographic shift: Middle-class and professional White families who once might have decamped to the suburbs began to raise their families in the city instead. The political clout of these families, combined with aggressive volunteer work, sometimes built effective schools in neighborhoods where they settled.

In New York City, crime began declining in the early 1990s, and, by 2000, the murder rate dropped to numbers not seen since the early 1960s. The subways, after years of neglect, were clean and functioning well. For some families, the suburbs had lost their appeal.

The post-war suburbs were built at a time when mothers (at least White mothers) mostly stayed home and fathers left the office promptly at 5:00 P.M., when people married young and had large families, when gasoline was cheap, and traffic moved smoothly. But that began to change as more women entered the labor force and both men and women worked longer hours; gas became more expensive; and traffic got worse. Delayed age of marriage and smaller families made it possible to stay in small city apartments and forgo large houses in the suburbs. (9) These changes fueled what journalist Alan Ehrenhalt calls "The Great Inversion"—the migration of the educated elite to city centers and the migration of poor and working class to the cities' periphery and suburbs, reversing the trends of the second half of the 20th century.

Of course, for many families weighing whether to live in the city or the suburbs, the quality of schools was (and still is) the deciding factor. In the 1990s, many city schools had dilapidated buildings and inadequate supplies, and suburban schools looked like country clubs in comparison. Teacher salaries were higher in the suburbs; class sizes were smaller. The city's schools were rapidly losing talented staff. Some 113 principals left in summer of 1998, most for jobs in the suburbs where salaries were $20,000 to $25,000 higher and working conditions easier. (10)

For middle-class and professional White parents raising their children in Brooklyn, city life had great appeal—but for the cash-strapped public schools. These parents began to lobby for special programs that would insulate their children from the worst disadvantages of the public school system. Some sought out "gifted" programs—tracked classes within ordinary neighborhood schools. Others rejected what they saw as the rigidity of traditional education and started from scratch—creating alternative schools within the public system.

Just as Chinese immigrants were able to make the best of inadequate public schools by supplementing with private test prep, middle-class and professional White parents compensated for poorly funded public education with aggressive organizing, volunteer work, and PTA fundraising. These efforts, however well-meaning, put high-poverty schools at a disadvantage. Even if their school budgets are comparable, high-poverty schools can't compete with schools that rely on the considerable resources of middle-class parents.

For example, in 1987, a group of parents in District 15, which includes both gentrified Park Slope and the working-class neighborhoods of Sunset Park and Red Hook, persuaded their local school board to let them open an alternative program, called Brooklyn New School, in an unused annex of PS 27 in Red Hook, surrounded by public housing projects. They recruited their own teachers, paid for supplies with their own money, and embraced a progressive approach to education that valued children's voices. Children called teachers by their first names. Class trips formed the basis of the curriculum. Parents were not only welcome in the classroom, they were encouraged to help out. Even before the school opened, parents cleared out garbage from the classrooms, sanded and painted old tables, built bookshelves, and sewed their own curtains. A carpenter father built bookshelves. A journalist mother helped children write their own books. (11)

Brooklyn New School parents weren't seeking out segregated education. Indeed, the school was proudly integrated, with a weighted lottery for admission to ensure a racial balance—one-third Black, one-third Latino, and one-third White or other. More than half were from low-income families. But in a school system that overwhelmingly served low-income Black and Latino children, a school that was one-third White and that had a significant number of middle-class families was seen as an island of privilege. Just as important, the school had the advantage of enrolling children whose parents wanted them to be there.

"They didn't want parents who would just kind of leave their kids at the door and not be involved," said Pamela Wheaton, my friend and colleague whose daughters attended Brooklyn New School in the 1990s. "You had to visit the school, you had to fill out a separate application. So, if you just didn't know about it, then you wouldn't apply. Parents in the know would get in." Pamela would help me create the InsideSchools website in 2001 as a way to give all parents access to information that had previously been the province of insiders.

Brooklyn New School outgrew the PS 27 annex and moved, first to another shared space and then to its own building. As its popularity grew, the leadership of District 15 opened other alternative schools and modified the teaching style at the ordinary neighborhood schools to reflect the progressive philosophy many middle-class White parents preferred. Desks in rows were out. Comfy sofas and rugs were in. Textbooks were replaced with fun-to-read picture books.

Under the direction of Carmen Fariña, who became superintendent of District 15 in 2001 (and who would serve as Mayor Bill de Blasio's schools chancellor from 2014 to 2018), schools that had once served overwhelmingly low-income Black and Latino children began to attract families of different races and income levels. Fariña paired successful schools with those that were struggling. She encouraged teachers and principals to visit other schools to share successful ideas and techniques. The quality of schools throughout the district improved. The number of White and Asian children in the elementary schools more than doubled from 2005 to 2019. Enrollments surged.

At a few schools, hyperactive PTAs began to raise astonishing amounts of money, with budgets sometimes topping $1 million a year. Schools that once were models of diversity now seemed to be bastions of White privilege.

To be sure, these super-wealthy schools represented a tiny percentage of the public school system. But the contrast between schools that were overwhelmingly White and those that had almost no White students seemed ever starker.

For Black parents—both U.S. born and immigrants from the West Indies—school options were more limited than those of White families in neighborhoods like Park Slope or Asian families in neighborhoods like Bensonhurst. In many White neighborhoods, Black families were unwelcome—the murder of a Black teenager trying to buy a used car in Bensonhurst in 1989 was a reminder of that, if one was needed. Instead, most Black families settled in historically Black neighborhoods with struggling schools.

Continuing housing discrimination combined with the legacy of redlining (and the decision to place most public housing and homeless shelters in low-income, majority Black neighborhoods) means that Black families, whatever their income, are more likely to live in neighborhoods with concentrated poverty than White people, including poor White people. (12) As a result, Black children tend to be assigned to high-poverty schools. These schools tend to have inexperienced teachers, rote instruction, and high rates of absenteeism—difficult barriers for children to overcome. (13) Some high-poverty schools with exceptionally strong leaders have overcome these barriers. But they are rare.

On average, public schools are most successful when they enroll a critical mass of children, whatever their race, from middle-class families. It's not that middle-class children are smarter, or harder working, or more deserving than anyone else. But low-income children are more likely to begin school without a strong preschool experience. They are at higher risk for homelessness and health problems such as asthma that make them miss school. Poor attendance, combined with poor preparation, leads to lower academic performance, not only for the children who miss school but also for their classmates: Teachers tend to slow the pace of instruction to let the children who are behind catch up.

Middle-income children, with stronger preschool experience, more stable housing, and better health, begin school with stronger math and reading skills and tend to have better attendance. Middle-income parents, who may have higher levels of education, more free time, and more disposable income, are more able to help with homework and offer out-of-school enrichment and tutoring. These efforts free up teachers' time to work with children who need extra attention. Decades of research have confirmed that schools with a mix of children from different family incomes are, on average, more successful than schools that only serve low-income children. Poor children as well as middle-class children tend to perform better in economically mixed schools.

Race and class are intertwined in the United States. Schools with high proportions of Black and Latino children also tend to be high-poverty schools. That's one reason why it's so hard for majority Black and Latino schools to succeed.

"While racial segregation is important, it's not the race of one's classmates that matters," says Stanford economist Sean Reardon, an expert on the impact of racial and economic school segregation. "It's the fact that in America today, racial segregation brings with it very unequal concentrations of students in high- and low-poverty schools." (14)

In the 1990s, nearly all the schools in Bedford-Stuyvesant's District 16 were weighed down by the problems that high concentrations of poverty bring. PS 304—housed in the building that would later become Brighter Choice—was one of the lowest performing in the city, with just 12% of children reading at grade level in 1995. PS 304 had four principals in 4 years. The school had no PTA. Parents and administrators squabbled, and some of the best-trained teachers left. (15)

In a few cases, extremely talented principals were able to beat the odds. For example, PS 21, Crispus Attucks School, was an orderly, no-nonsense place with high expectations, where girls wore burgundy plaid jumpers and boys wore burgundy plaid ties. Principal Renee Young, a dynamic and effective leader, modeled PS 21 after the parochial school she attended herself as a child, and her school was a favorite among parents. But even successful schools like PS 21 faced headwinds from the education bureaucracy. Unlike the principals of parochial schools, Young was not allowed to hire her own staff. Instead, officials told me when I visited in the mid-1990s, she was vulnerable to the caprices of the school board, who would remove and reassign her best teachers to other schools.

The community school board—originally designed to give a small measure of community control of schools—was mired in political infighting and mismanagement. District 16 school board members were suspended three times in the 1990s. In one case, two school board members were arrested after they got into a shoving match; in another, a board member brandished a knife at another member; in the third case, the board was suspended after becoming deadlocked over the choice of a superintendent.

Then and now, many Bedford-Stuyvesant parents voted with their feet, enrolling their children in private schools or in public schools in adjacent districts. Black parents, both African American and West Indian immigrants, were often willing to send their children on long commutes for a good education—as Keesha had done. Through word of mouth, Black parents sought out pockets of academic excellence in neighborhoods where Black residents were welcome. One such school was PS 235, several miles south of Bedford-Stuyvesant in East Flatbush, called Little Caribbean because it was home to many West Indian immigrants. When I visited in the mid-1990s, PS 235 had a strong and thoughtful principal, Mitchel Levine, effective teachers, and a large gifted program that attracted children from across Brooklyn and even from other boroughs. Parents who worked at nearby Kings County Hospital commuted with their children; others paid for a private bus service. While other schools in Black neighborhoods had trouble filling their seats, PS 235 had more than 1,400 pupils, spread over three buildings.

Nearly all the children at PS 235 were Black, and two thirds were poor enough to qualify for free lunch. Yet the school had many involved parents, including a solid core of middle-class parents. Some parents accompanied their children to the library on weekends and managed to find time to volunteer as tutors, to chaperone class trips, and to act as security guards during the day. Parents ran an after-school program with lessons in dance, computers, science, and arts and crafts. Strong leadership, high academic expectations, and parent involvement have built a strong community for all the children at PS 235.

PS 235 in East Flatbush attracts children from a mix of family incomes, and that partly accounts for its success. But, in the 1990s, most of the ordinary neighborhood schools in Bedford-Stuyvesant's District 16 were overwhelmed by the heavy weight of poverty and wracked by the district's poor leadership and political infighting.

By the end of the 20th century, White and Asian children in Brooklyn, including those who were poor, increasingly had access to schools with effective leadership, strong teaching, and classmates from a range of family incomes. The schools in Districts 20 and 15, in particular, had emerged from the troubled years of the 1980s with a sense of optimism and purpose. But many schools in Brooklyn's Black and Latino neighborhoods continued to struggle, and the improvements in schools in White and Asian neighborhoods only served to heighten the growing inequality and unfairness of the system: Increasingly, White and Asian parents could simply register their children at their zoned neighborhood elementary schools and be confident of a good education, while Black and Latino parents were forced either to enroll their children at inadequate schools near home or scramble for admission to distant schools that offered more opportunities. The school system reinforced racial inequality. Schools in Black and Latino neighborhoods, drained of the most active parents who could help support them, struggled with the impact of declining enrollments and high concentrations of poverty. The children leaving those schools, meanwhile, endured punishing commutes—not to mention the hostility they often faced in majority White schools.

Across the country in the 1990s, even as White Americans were beginning to move back to urban centers, public schools were becoming more racially and economically segregated. A 1999 report by Gary Orfield at Harvard University's Civil Rights Project found that Black and Latino children's contact with White students in school had been decreasing for a decade, in large part the result of U.S. Supreme Court decisions, beginning in 1991, that freed school districts from desegregation orders.

But few people were paying attention. News of Orfield's report was tucked on p. 41 of *The New York Times* with a dismissive quote from Chester E. Finn, Jr., a fellow at the conservative Hudson Institute.

"Gary Orfield must be the only American who still thinks that integration for its own sake is an important societal goal," the *Times* quoted Finn as saying. "Almost everybody else is interested in whether kids are going to good schools where they are safe and learning to read. The price of forced busing and other forms of social engineering is too high to pay when there are more urgent crises facing this country's schools." (16)

Finn, of course, misses the point. Civil rights activists did not argue for integration for its own sake—however beneficial it may be for children of different races to learn to get along with one another. For Galamison, the organizer of the 1964 school boycott, integration was a means to an end: equality in education. For researchers like Reardon, integration is a way to ensure that low-income children aren't isolated in high-poverty schools, schools that are almost always overwhelmed by the troubles that very poor children, through no fault of their own, bring to class. To be sure, all-Black schools, like PS 235, can be successful. But mixing children of different family incomes, as PS 235 does, is part of their success. And in America today, because poverty is racialized, racial integration and mixing children of different family incomes usually go hand in hand.

As the courts released school districts from racial desegregation orders, many districts abandoned attempts at school integration (although successful school desegregation programs continued, particularly in the South and in a few progressive cities in the North). As income inequality grew, the rich increasingly lived with other rich people, the poor with other poor people, and the number of people living in mixed-income neighborhoods declined. The country's schools were increasingly segregated both by race and class. (17)

The country seemed resigned to segregation, and political leaders looked for ways to improve education for low-income Black and Latino children without addressing racial and income inequality. A political climate that endorsed market-based solutions to social problems favored policies of school choice as a mechanism for achieving school improvement. According to the marketplace model, schools would compete for enrollment and resources. Weaker schools would falter when they failed to attract students. Less preferred schools would need to close or emulate the programs of more successful schools to stay in business. The stronger schools would offer better options for more children.

In New York City in the early years of the 21st century, the creation of hundreds of new schools and the rapid expansion school choice under Mayor Michael Bloomberg offered new opportunities to many New York City children. But these policies failed to close the gap between haves and have-nots and even exacerbated the racial and economic segregation that was already entrenched in the city's schools. Brighter Choice, along with other new schools founded in the Bloomberg years, would reflect both the promise and the limitations of the city's most ambitious school reform efforts in decades.

FOUR

The Promise and Pitfalls of School Choice

courtesy of InsideSchools.org

Ms. Fabayo's school flourished as choice expanded, but others didn't fare as well.

Fabayo McIntosh, who grew up in Bedford-Stuyvesant and attended Little Sun People as a child in the 1980s, had her work cut out for her when she opened Brighter Choice Community School in 2008. Not only did Ms. Fabayo, as the new principal was called, need to hire teachers, buy books and supplies, and design a curriculum, she also had to recruit parents who would take a chance on a new school, housed in a building and a district with a negative reputation.

"I had to knock on doors to get kids to come into the building," she recalled later. "I literally scavenged the neighborhood, the projects and everything, knocking on doors. The police were like, 'Miss, you're crazy. Don't do this.' But at that time, I needed students." (1)

Brighter Choice was part of Mayor Mike Bloomberg's sweeping initiative to create better options for children in low-income neighborhoods, closing more than 160 low-performing schools and opening more than 600 new ones in their place—the biggest upheaval to the New York City school system in decades. Ms. Fabayo was one of hundreds of new leaders who would shake up the school system and vastly expand the city's system of school choice.

Ms. Fabayo, like Mama Fela, had studied at Bank Street College of Education. Consistent with the Bank Street ethos, Ms. Fabayo had a vision of a school that would offer imaginative lessons to spark children's curiosity—not the scripted curriculum that's typical of high-poverty schools. She wanted Brighter Choice to give children the same love of African American culture and pride in their heritage that she received as a child at Little Sun People. "Little Sun People was my foundation," Ms. Fabayo told me one afternoon as we sat on a park bench in Lower Manhattan near the central offices of the Department of Education, where she was assigned after leaving Brighter Choice. "Everything was done through the lens of 'Black is beautiful.'"

She recruited teachers who shared her vision and were willing to work long hours, but finding children to fill the seats at Brighter Choice was a challenge. The new school was housed in a building, constructed in 1962, that had been home to PS 304, one of the lowest-performing schools in the city. Surrounded by public housing developments, in the vicinity of three shelters for homeless families and for victims of domestic violence, PS 304 served a vulnerable and transient population. Because of its low test scores, under the provisions of No Child Left Behind, families were eligible to transfer their children to other schools. Many did. There was a shortage of teachers willing to work at PS 304. Older students sometimes led classes if the principal couldn't find substitutes for absent teachers.

"The school was out of control," a PS 304 graduate named Latisha posted on the InsideSchools website, recalling her days as a pupil in 2003. "It was a kid's worst nightmare. There were fights most every day. Girls in the 5th grade would tease and jump this young Muslim girl and no one did anything to help."

The Department of Education closed PS 304 in 2008. Ms. Fabayo's task would be to persuade prospective parents that her new school would be different.

Mayor Bloomberg, who took office in 2002, firmly believed that decentralization and the community school boards, in place since 1969, had failed children, particularly Black and Latino children in neighborhoods like Bedford-Stuyvesant. Only centralized control, under the mayor, he argued, could guarantee equity and rid the schools of the patronage, corruption, and mismanagement that plagued too many community school boards. The quality of a child's education, he said, should not depend on their zip code.

In Bloomberg's vision, accountability and school choice in a marketplace of schools—not integration or community control—were the vehicles to drive reform. Parents were to be empowered with information about school quality (in the form of widely published student test scores) and offered the freedom to transfer their children out of low-performing schools. The power of the marketplace, it was assumed, would ensure that good schools would flourish, and bad schools would wither and die. His philosophy was in line with a national movement toward accountability and school choice, codified in the bipartisan 2002 No Child Left Behind Act designed to close the so-called "achievement gap" between poor Black and Latino children and their White and wealthier peers.

Bloomberg persuaded the state legislature to give him direct control of the city's schools, disbanding the community school boards while leaving the boundaries of the 32 districts in place. The new law gave him the power to hire—and fire—the school chancellor, who was previously appointed by an independent Board of Education. Under the new law, the mayor not only determined the size of the education budget, he also controlled how the money was spent. For the first time, the mayor had both responsibility for and authority over the city's schools.

The mayor hired as his school chancellor Joel Klein, a lawyer and Queens-born public-school graduate best known for his anti-trust work with the U.S. Justice Department against Microsoft. The symbolism was clear: The Board of Education was an ossified monopoly that needed to be broken up, and a trustbuster who had battled the likes of Bill Gates was the man to do it—not a career educator. In another potent symbol, Bloomberg moved the Department of Education headquarters from downtown Brooklyn to the former Tweed Courthouse next to City Hall, where, it was understood, he could keep a close eye on it.

Bloomberg poured money into the schools, devoting billions of dollars to capital improvements and raising teacher salaries by 43%, making them competitive with suburban salaries for the first time in decades. During Bloomberg's administration the city's education budget would increase from $11.4 billion to $19.9 billion, the fortunate byproduct of mayoral control, the city's improving finances, and an infusion of state money from the settlement of a 1993 lawsuit that argued the state aid formula shortchanged the city's schools. (2)

No Child Left Behind required each state to give annual tests in reading and math to all children in grades 3 to 8; schools in which children failed to make adequate progress on the tests would face sanctions, including closure. New York State had long administered standardized tests, but now the stakes were high. In sync with the national mandate, Bloomberg and Klein put new emphasis on test scores, judging schools almost entirely by how well their students performed. They instituted an "A" to "F" grading system for schools and closed schools that didn't perform well.

PS 304 was one of the schools that got the ax. Two new schools took its place: Brighter Choice and another elementary school, Young Scholars Academy for Discovery and Exploration. The two schools shared a cafeteria, an auditorium, and a gym. They also shared a tiny attendance zone of just eight square blocks. (The building also housed a small school for disabled children, with its own principal and staff.) Parents living in the attendance zone could choose either Brighter Choice or Young Scholars—or they could apply to charter schools or traditional public schools nearby.

Competition for pupils was fierce. In 2008, there were seven other public schools within a half-mile radius of Brighter Choice—including Young Scholars in the same building. There were four charter schools—publicly funded, privately run—within a mile radius. A few miles away, there were several gifted programs and well-established neighborhood schools that recruited children from outside their attendance zones. To top it off, the number of school-age children in the neighborhood was declining. Families with children were being priced out of the neighborhood by rising rents. Many newcomers didn't have children, and those who did often sent them to private schools or to public schools outside the neighborhood.

To solve the riddle of how to fill the seats at her new school, Ms. Fabayo turned to the nursery school she had attended as a child and where her mother still worked. "Little Sun People was my secret weapon," she told me. When she recruited children from Little Sun People, she built a base of parents with shared values and culture. And, while Little Sun People was not expensive by private school standards, it did charge tuition, and, as a result, it had working- and middle-class parents who could bring energy and volunteer labor to the new school. Their children, having attended an excellent preschool, would be well prepared for elementary school.

Brighter Choice opened in the fall of 2008 with 70 pupils in prekindergarten through 2nd grade. In crucial ways, it was a beneficiary of Bloomberg's system of school choice. PS 304, with three homeless shelters nearby, had been overwhelmed by the problems that children in deep poverty bring to the school. Ms. Fabayo, on the other hand, was able to recruit families from outside the attendance zone whose energy helped support the school. Even as Brighter Choice continued to serve children from the nearby shelters, they made up a smaller proportion of the student body than they had at PS 304.

In its first years, Brighter Choice flourished and grew, adding grades until it served 150 children ranging from prekindergarten to 5th grade. Ms. Fabayo, who grew up around the corner from the school, stood outside each morning greeting children with hugs and hellos, as the InsideSchools website noted in 2013. She encouraged her staff to visit other successful schools, including a progressive charter school, Community Roots, which her own son attended. Building on her training from Bank Street College of Education and her knowledge of what children in her neighborhood need to be successful, Ms. Fabayo combined progressive and traditional teaching techniques to foster love of learning while ensuring children had basic skills. In math, for example, she combined hands-on methods (using small plastic blocks called manipulatives to solve problems) with regular drills and quizzes. In social studies, she drew on Bank Street's interdisciplinary curriculum: Each grade studied a different topic such as "transportation," or "family," or "Native Americans." Children would research these topics at the local library and take field trips to learn more. To encourage children to start thinking about higher education, 4th- and 5th-graders took trips to colleges, visiting dormitories and even sitting in on some classes.

In 2015, a whopping 70% of 4th-graders met state standards on the reading test, the highest percentage in District 16 and on par with schools in wealthier neighborhoods. Brighter Choice seemed to be beating the odds.

If Brighter Choice flourished thanks to the expansion of school choice under Mayor Bloomberg, most other schools in District 16 didn't fare as well. In fact, school choice, designed with the hope of bringing greater equity, further deepened the divide between schools that were functioning well and those that were struggling.

School choice allows parents to opt out of their local schools and, in Bedford-Stuyvesant, many did. Enrollment at the traditional, zoned neighborhood schools in District 16, which had decreased sharply during the decades of neighborhood abandonment and high crime, declined even further as charter schools opened and choice expanded.

Long gone were the days when Bedford-Stuyvesant schools were so crowded that children only attended school for 4 hours a day. By the time Bloomberg took office, schools built to house more than 1,000 children had fewer than 700. By the time he left office, some had fewer than 300. Shrinking enrollments make it more difficult for these schools to succeed.

If overcrowding brings one set of problems, under-enrollment brings another. High poverty schools with shrinking enrollments are caught in a downward spiral. City money is allocated according to the number of children in a school, and as their enrollments shrink, so do their budgets. As budgets shrink, schools are forced to lay off teachers and eliminate enrichment programs such as music and art—making them even less likely to attract new students in a competitive marketplace. And, during the Bloomberg administration, there was a Sword of Damocles over every school: the threat of being shut down if test scores or enrollments were too low.

The expansion of school choice under Bloomberg would have very different impacts on different neighborhoods. In neighborhoods with a large proportion of White and Asian residents, such as those in Brooklyn's Districts 15 and 20, parents are mostly satisfied with their zoned neighborhood schools; indeed, they buy expensive apartments or houses just so their children can attend the local schools. By and large, these parents don't take advantage of school choice. For them, they simply register their children at their zoned school with their proof of address.

On the other hand, parents in mostly Black and Hispanic neighborhoods, including changing neighborhoods like Bedford-Stuyvesant, tend to be less satisfied with their local schools. In District 16 in eastern Bedford-Stuyvesant, for example, more than two thirds of kindergarten parents opt out of their local schools. For these parents, school choice is both a blessing and a curse: an opportunity to escape a low-performing neighborhood school, but also a year-long bureaucratic gauntlet with multiple applications.

Applying to kindergarten can be a grueling process in New York City. Parents considering "gifted" programs, for example, must sign up in November for their children to be tested in January—fully 8 months before the school year begins. Ordinary neighborhood schools admit children from outside their attendance zones if there is room—but parents must submit an application ranking their choices in January, and the most popular schools are oversubscribed. Charter schools are yet another option—but parents need to apply for a lottery in April.

Racial Dynamics of School Choice in Brooklyn

Families in mostly Black and Hispanic neighborhoods opt out more.

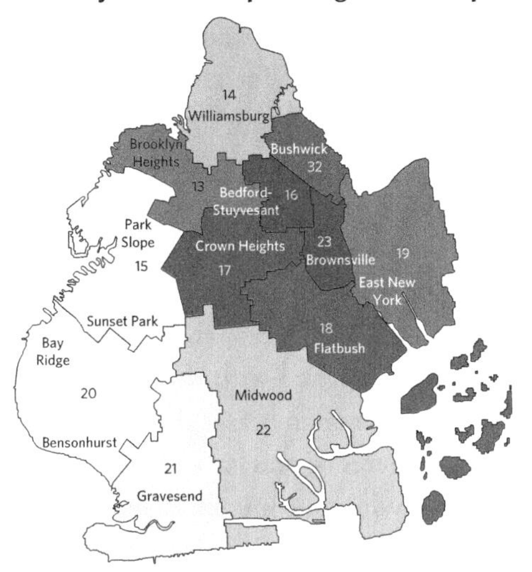

Percent of Black and Hispanic Kindergartners 2016-2017

% 40 60 80

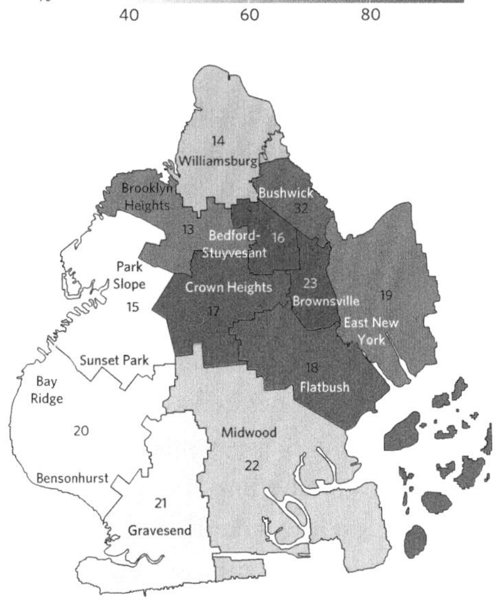

Percent of Kindergartners Opting Out of District 2016-2017

% 20 40 60

Source: "Paradox of Choice", Nicole Mader, Center for NYC Affairs

Neighborhood dynamics of school choice: Families in mostly Black and Hispanic neighborhoods opt out more.

The system isn't designed for parents who show up the first day of school, hoping to enroll their child, or who arrive midyear. For these parents, choice is usually limited to their zoned neighborhood school—the only place required to make room for children regardless of when they enroll. Lower-income families who move frequently may not know in the spring where they will be living in the fall; if they wait to register on the first day of classes, their default option is their zoned school. Similarly, if they move during the school year, their only option is often their zoned school.

The ideology driving school choice—the power of the invisible hand of the marketplace—was not designed with the intent of separating children by race and income level, but in many cases that's what happened. That's because school choice favors parents who have the time and energy to research their options. While many low-income families take advantage of school choice, most parents who don't speak English, or who are homeless, or who are simply unaware of their options, do not.

Bloomberg didn't invent school choice. Indeed, New York City has long had an informal system of school choice. The city's density means many schools are within walking distance; the extensive subway system means children can travel outside their neighborhood even if busing isn't available. At the most basic level, parents have lied about their addresses to enroll in better schools for at least 100 years. In Betty Smith's semi-autobiographical novel, *A Tree Grows in Brooklyn,* set in the early 20th century, the main character transfers to a better school by lying about her address.

But by the 1990s, when I began visiting schools, school choice was an unruly patchwork: each of the city's 32 school districts had its own rules about how to apply. Each district operated as its own fiefdom, trying to lure the best students from other districts—while making it next to impossible for its own children to find out anything about schools outside its borders. Some schools required children to take their own in-house exam; others looked for children with artistic talent; still others wanted parents who were willing to volunteer.

As Bloomberg's school chancellor, Klein codified the admission rules, seeking to limit entitled parents' use of influence to get their children into the most desirable schools—and the ability of districts to poach the best students. Standardized, transparent admissions procedures would level the playing field, he believed. But, while his stated purpose was to ensure fairness and guarantee that the quality of a child's education was not determined by their address, some of his policies had the unintended effect of further dividing children by race and class.

Klein's policy on admissions to "gifted" programs is an example of how a policy designed to ensure fairness backfired. Klein believed that a system that allowed each principal to determine entrance requirements was open to favoritism. In attempt to centralize and standardize a hodgepodge of different programs, the Klein administration created one citywide entrance exam for 4-year-olds applying to kindergarten gifted programs. No longer were there different tests with different deadlines, measuring different aptitudes, in different neighborhoods. To be considered for admission, children had to score in the 90th percentile—or, depending on the program, the 97th percentile—on a nationally normed test, that is, one designed to rank children nationwide. The test was given in January or February the year before children started kindergarten.

Before Klein's policies took effect, a low-income Black or Latino child from the Bronx who was academically far ahead of his neighborhood peers (but not necessarily in the tippy-top nationwide) could test into a gifted program based on the admissions requirements of a particular school. Now the same child had to get a top score on a nationally normed test—essentially forced to compete with rich White kids from the Upper East Side, who may have already had several years of private nursery school as well as private tutoring and coaching for the test.

Gifted programs in mostly White neighborhoods and in mixed neighborhoods flourished, but the city forced most of the gifted programs in Black and Latino neighborhoods to close because only a handful of children scored high enough to meet the new national standards.

One gifted program that served mostly Black children somehow dodged the city's mandate to centralize admissions: PS 235, the giant elementary school that attracted families from across Brooklyn to the neighborhood known as Little Caribbean in East Flatbush. Flying under the Department of Education radar, PS 235 named its classes for advanced students SOAR (Stimulating Outstanding Achievement Through Reading). It admitted out-of-district children according to the results of an exam given by the school, as it had done for years. Based on its longstanding reputation, it continued to be a sought-after, high-performing school, even after the SOAR program was discontinued in 2019.

Whether any elementary school should divide children into "gifted" and not-gifted classes, is, of course a legitimate question. New York City's policy of testing 4-year-olds for "giftedness" is the subject of much well-founded criticism. But, if a city is to have gifted programs, they should serve Black and Hispanic as well as White and Asian children.

When Bloomberg centralized admission to gifted programs, the proportion of White children grew significantly. While White students made up just 16% of the city's public-school enrollment, the proportion of White children in gifted programs grew from 33% to 48% in 2008, the first year the new admissions test was introduced. There were just 16,000 seats in gifted programs—a tiny number in a city with 1.1 million students. Yet the racial disparities were a potent symbol of an unequal system. (3)

The ideology of school choice also led to the expansion of charter schools in New York City. Their enrollments exploded from barely 3,000 in 2002 to 70,000 in 2014, when Bloomberg left office. By 2021, they served 145,000 children. Unlike the gifted programs, the new charter schools were mostly located in low-income Black and Latino neighborhoods. And unlike gifted programs, charter schools were open to all by lottery—with no entrance exam required.

Yet the charter schools, too, deepened the class divide in the school system, separating the very poorest children from those whose families were a little more financially stable. Because the admission lottery for charters is held in April, they tend to enroll families with stable housing—who know in the spring where they are going to live in the fall. Traditional public schools enroll children year-round, and those who arrive midyear tend to have more academic struggles than those who start the year on time. Traditional public schools tend to have higher proportions of homeless children, more children who don't speak English, and more children who need special education services. Most charters are committed to serving low-income children, but they tend to enroll fewer of the most vulnerable children than the district schools do.

Consider Bedford-Stuyvesant's Excellence Girls Charter School, which opened in 2009 with a kindergarten and 1st-grade class in a building shared with PS 309, a zoned neighborhood school in District 16. The charter school, with a mission to "empower" girls, had a demanding curriculum, an extra-long school day, and a focus on building character. Within a few years,

Excellence Girls had some of the highest test scores in the state. In 2016, the U.S. Department of Education honored it as Blue Ribbon School, an award given for academic excellence. Schools Chancellor Carmen Fariña praised the school's "passionate teachers and eager students."

But staff members at PS 309, the zoned neighborhood school in the same building, maintained that the charter school served a different, easier-to-reach population. The poverty rate at both schools was almost the same—roughly three in four students at both schools qualified for free lunch. But PS 309 had more children who were still learning English, and more children who received special education services. Most telling, some 20% of the children at PS 309 were living in temporary housing, compared to 7% of the children at Excellence Girls. The administration at Excellence Girls, committed to equity, gave preference in admission to homeless children. Nonetheless, more children in temporary housing wound up at PS 309.

The largest and best-known of the charter school organizations is Success Academy, which operates 47 schools serving 20,000 students in New York City. Known for sky-high test scores and strict discipline, Success Academy is a lightning rod for both supporters and critics of the charter school movement. An analysis by education writer Robert Pondisco finds Success Academy owes its success not to cherry-picking students but cherry-picking *parents,* requiring unusual levels of parent involvement and making constant demands on their time. Others have criticized Success Academy for limiting enrollment of students with special needs, forcing out underachievers, and failing to fill empty seats. (4)

Charter schools may have drawn the most controversy during the Bloomberg administration, but Klein's reforms also had a profound effect on the ordinary public schools, particularly at the high school level. Klein's most ambitious initiative, beginning in 2002, was the creation of hundreds of new small high schools, thanks to $500 million in grants from several foundations (including the Gates Foundation—a sign that Bill Gates had no hard feelings about Klein's lawsuit against Microsoft).

These small schools offered the individual attention that was missing at large schools and had the benefit of retaining students who might otherwise have dropped out. The small schools were largely responsible for the dramatic increase in the city's graduation rate from 51% in 2002 to 66% in 2013, according to research by respected firms such as MDRC. But, as other researchers have observed, they also had the unintended effect of further dividing high school students by race and class. (5)

Bloomberg inherited a complex and unequal system that included some of the best (or at least most renowned) high schools in the country as well as some of the worst. At the top of the pecking order, at least in terms of prestige, were the specialized schools, with admission by a competitive exam: Stuyvesant High School, Brooklyn Technical High School, and Bronx High School of Science. (Four more exam schools, in the works before Bloomberg was elected, opened in 2002.) At the bottom were most of the traditional zoned high schools, dubbed "dropout factories," which were often unruly, even violent places.

In between were highly selective schools such as Townsend Harris High School in Queens; dozens of alternative schools (such as John Dewey, which Keesha attended in the 1980s); several performing arts schools, including LaGuardia High School of Music and Art and Performing Arts; and well-regarded vocational schools such as Aviation High School (which trains airplane mechanics).

In the early 1990s, about 40 small schools had opened with the support of the Annenberg and Carnegie foundations. In addition, frustrated by the low quality of high schools governed by the central Board of Education, some local school districts (which governed elementary and middle schools) took it on themselves to open high schools for their own students. In all, the city had some 200 high schools at the beginning of Bloomberg's mayoralty, ranging in size from the tiny Urban Academy in Manhattan, with just 100 pupils, to the gigantic Brooklyn Tech, with more than 4,000.

Bloomberg and Klein determined that the best way to boost the city's stagnant graduation rates was to close large, dysfunctional neighborhood high schools and replace them with small, themed schools. Their conclusion was in line with research by the Boston-based Parthenon Group that found student–teacher ratios and teacher salaries were *not* statistically significant predictors of graduation rates, but school size and the concentration of low-performing students *were* significant predictors.

In place of the large high schools, some of which had enrollments of more than 4,000, the city opened several hundred new schools with just

400 students each. Five or more schools, each with a theme like "sports management" or "film and music," would share a large building; each school had its own floor or wing and its own principal and staff. With a smaller class size (28 versus 34) and a smaller enrollment overall, these schools offered students far more individual attention. As the anonymity of the giant buildings yielded to the intimacy of a community where every teacher knew the name of every student, schools became safer.

Citywide, fewer than one third of students entering 9th grade were reading at grade level in 2002, and many of the students who had attended the dysfunctional high schools were 3 or 4 years behind. Accordingly, most of the new, smaller schools focused their resources on intense remediation to ensure that the weakest students could graduate within 4 years. Indeed, the new schools were much more successful at retaining and graduating low-performing students than the "dropout factories" they replaced. However, because of their small enrollments and budgets, these schools could not offer *both* the remedial classes that so many children needed *and* the college-prep classes such as chemistry and physics that stronger students wanted (and that middle-class parents demanded).

This tension between the small schools' admirable focus on helping students who were far behind in their studies and the growing demand for schools with a college-preparatory curriculum led the city to create separate schools for students with different skills levels, often within the same building. Because low-income Black and Latino students were more likely to need remedial help, these schools were also divided by race and class. High achieving students, mostly White and Asian, were clustered in a small number of schools; lower achieving students, mostly Black and Latino, were in the rest.

Take the case of John Jay High School in posh Park Slope. Housed in a once-elegant five-story building, opened in 1902, John Jay had declined in the 1970s, like many other city schools. As Park Slope gentrified in the 1980s and 1990s, middle-class and professional parents willingly sent their children to the elementary school, PS 321, across the street, and to the middle school, MS 51, a few blocks away. But they avoided John Jay, choosing private high schools or public schools outside the neighborhood. John Jay was known as a crime-ridden school of last resort, serving mostly low-income Black and Latino students from outside the neighborhood. The building's roof was leaky, walls were moldy, and lockers were filled with garbage and mice.

The city closed John Jay in 2004, and three small schools moved in. The small schools that replaced John Jay were an improvement: They graduated about 70% of their pupils on time—twice as many as the old John Jay. But discipline problems continued, and attendance was poor. Two of the three schools had rapid turnover of principals and bare-bones curricula. (One had stable leadership and offered physics and calculus.) Most graduates were not prepared for college—and had to take remedial classes if they attended the City University of New York. The building, which had metal detectors and surly security guards at the entrance, continued to serve almost entirely low-income Black and Latino children from outside the neighborhood.

Then in 2010, Park Slope parents began agitating for a new high school. Selective public schools in Manhattan that had once accepted children from Brooklyn, including one called Millennium High School, no longer had room. Why not create a clone of Millennium in the old John Jay, the Park Slope parents asked? There was plenty of room—the small schools had trouble recruiting students. Klein, the school chancellor, agreed, and Millennium Brooklyn opened in 2011.

Newspapers called the new school "elite," but its admission requirements were modest: Applicants were expected to have an 85 average and score Level 3 or 4 on 4-level standardized tests—that is, meet the state's standards for academic achievement. The first class of 9th-graders was one-third White, with the remainder evenly split among Black, Latino, and Asian students. About 40% were from low-income families. The new school integrated pupils on the autism spectrum into its regular classes.

Nonetheless, Millennium Brooklyn seemed like an island of privilege in the old John Jay, where there were no admissions requirements, just 5 percent of the children were White, and 85 percent were low income. Students at the existing small schools resented the fact that Millennium got extra startup money for renovations, that it had extensive sports teams (including fencing and table tennis) when the John Jay kids couldn't even field a soccer team. "It felt like our kids were being kicked to the curb while the Millennium kids were given preference," a John Jay parent told *New York Magazine*. "It just wasn't fair." (6) Bringing White children into a building where none had been for years didn't create segregation and inequality—both had plagued the city for decades. But concentrating White children in one small school made segregation and inequality visible and obvious in a way it had not been in the years of high crime and abandonment, when all schools had been equally blighted.

By the end of Bloomberg's mayoralty, many of the city's schools had rebounded from the dark days of the 1970s and 1980s. More students were graduating from high school. With the opening of new high schools, high-achieving students had more options for a college prep curriculum and lower-achieving students had a better chance of remediation. Schools were safer. With more funding, there were more books and supplies. Schools like Brighter Choice offered better options than the schools they replaced. Teachers were better paid—and less likely to leave for jobs in the suburbs. Expenditures per student, adjusted for inflation, grew from $15,140 in 2004 to $18,620 in 2012. (7)

But the gaps between the haves and the have-nots were as wide as ever. While graduation rates increased for all racial groups, the rates for Black and Latino students continued to lag. Racial disparities among New York City's 4th- and 8th-graders on nationally normed tests remained unchanged from 2002 to 2015, according to an analysis by New York University researcher Norm Fruchter. School choice and the accountability measures of No Child Left Behind had failed to close the gap in school outcomes between Black and Latino children and their White and Asian peers. (8)

Bloomberg had begun his first term just months after the terrorist attacks of Sept. 11, 2001, killed 3,000 people and rattled the city. Unemployment was high and tax revenues were declining. To bring the city back, he gave tax breaks to spur a high-end building boom and added amenities that would make people—especially the wealthy—want to live in New York City. "Get enough rich people and companies here, and they will support a government that can keep the city running for everyone else," *Times* columnist Jim Dwyer wrote. (9)

The mayor succeeded in attracting the rich. But skyrocketing prices made it harder for everyone else to live in New York. Inequality, which had been growing for years, accelerated during his mayoralty. According to an analysis by economist James Parrott, in 1980, the top 1% of New Yorkers had 12% of the city's income. By 2015, the top 1% had nearly 40% of the city's income. (10)

By the end of Bloomberg's time in office, many parents and teachers had tired of the relentless emphasis on test scores to judge children and their schools, the constant threat of school closures, and the competition among schools that choice had fostered—not to mention the high cost of housing.

Bloomberg's successor, Bill de Blasio, campaigned to end inequality in the city and what he called "The Tale of Two Cities"—the fortunes of the richest New Yorkers and everyone else. He promised to offer prekindergarten to all 4-year-olds in the city, with some 70,000 seats, citing research that said it was one of the "most effective means of reducing income inequality, increasing social mobility, raising college graduation rates, reducing crime, and increasing wages." (11)

The expansion of prekindergarten would be de Blasio's biggest accomplishment, but he would make little progress tackling the growing inequality in the city. The fortunes of the rich continued to rise. Housing prices climbed into the stratosphere. Poor and working-class people were hurt the most, but even people with good salaries were squeezed by the high cost of housing.

Middle-class and professional White parents, priced out of neighborhoods with "good" schools (or at least schools with high test scores), began to move into Bedford-Stuyvesant. Their arrival would spark conflicts as newcomers and long-time residents struggled to share space in the neighborhood and, particularly, in the local schools.

FIVE

◇◇◇◇◇◇◇◇◇◇◇◇◇◇◇◇◇◇◇◇◇◇◇◇◇◇◇◇◇◇

How Gentrification Brought Conflict

courtesy of InsideSchools.org

A new force in the neighborhood: The Bed-Stuy Parents Committee.

In 2015, a group of newcomers to Bedford-Stuyvesant, including many White parents, decided they wanted to send their children to local schools—rather than outside the neighborhood. Shaila Dewan, a reporter for *The New York Times*, was one of the founders of the group that would come to be known as The Bed-Stuy Parents Committee.

"I thought, 'Why can't Bed-Stuy have what other neighborhoods have?'" Shaila, who is of mixed White and Asian ancestry, told an interviewer for the podcast School Colors. "Why am I going to take my kid to Clinton Hill or Fort Greene or to lower Manhattan? My God, I mean there are parents here that take their kids to the Lower East Side [in Manhattan] for school. That just outraged me. Like this is not insurmountable. Like we should be able to have here what everybody else has." (1)

Shaila was saying out loud what many parents thought: Parents in White and Asian neighborhoods could mostly count on their local schools; parents in Black and Latino neighborhoods, not so much. Now, as White parents moved to neighborhoods like Bedford-Stuyvesant, they were discovering a harsh reality; inequality did not only hurt poor Black and Latino children, it could hurt their own children as well. The only people who benefited from this inequality were those who could afford to live in the most expensive neighborhoods.

In theory, this realization could have led to solidarity between the White newcomers and the long-time Black community activists, an alliance to fight for better schools for all. But the two groups would need to build trust, understanding, and mutual respect—qualities in short supply in changing neighborhoods like Bedford-Stuyvesant.

By the 1990s, gentrification had spread from the mostly White neighborhoods of Park Slope and Brooklyn Heights to historically Black neighborhoods of Brownstone Brooklyn, as the areas with stunning 19th-century architecture are known. The first gentrifiers were Black: Fort Greene and Clinton Hill, historically poor African American neighborhoods with tree-lined streets and gracious if run-down row houses, became a magnet for Black artists and musicians, with residents like actor Laurence Fishburne, filmmaker Spike Lee, rapper Common, and saxophonist Branford Marsalis. Elegant brownstones were renovated. Black entrepreneurs opened restaurants and shops. (2)

By the beginning of the 21st century, gentrification had pushed east to Bedford-Stuyvesant, the heart of Black culture and pride. White residents, pushed out by rapidly rising rents in other neighborhoods, began to move in as well. Like Fort Greene and Clinton Hill before, townhouses in Bedford-Stuyvesant were renovated. Bike lanes appeared. Trendy cafes and expensive restaurants opened. The population of Bedford-Stuyvesant grew

15% between 2000 and 2017; housing prices tripled; the proportion of White residents grew from less than 3% to nearly 27%. (3) As White residents moved in, Black residents left, among them renters pushed out by rising costs; elderly homeowners cashing in on rising prices to retire in the South; and young families moving to the suburbs of Long Island or New Jersey to raise their children.

For some long-time residents like Mama Fela, the changes were just as frightening as the years of high crime. Although the brownstone she purchased in 1990 for $195,000 had skyrocketed in value, she increasingly felt out of place on her own block. She used to buy coffee at a "hole in the wall." Now, the only coffee is at an upscale place where it costs $3. The neighborhood used to have block parties that went until 11 or 12 o'clock at night, with the kids playing and the grown-ups talking and playing music. Now, if there's any noise after 7:00 P.M. the cops come and send everyone home. She feels her neighborhood is no longer the refuge for Black households—even a refuge troubled by crime and poverty—that it had been for decades.

"About 15 years ago I started seeing the first people who were not Black, and I felt all kinds of horrible bad feelings," she told me in 2019. "Every time I would come out of my house, I would be so angry."

She felt powerless, swept along by a tide of wealth and power. As she spoke to me, her eyes filled with tears. "I apologize for the tears but it's really hard for me to talk about Bed-Stuy without falling apart."

Gentrification is often "dreaded and welcomed at the same time by the same people," writes sociologist Lance Freeman. Long-time residents may be optimistic and receptive to neighborhood change, and, simultaneously, pessimistic and distrustful. They welcome amenities such as pharmacies, supermarkets, and restaurants. Municipal services, such as street repairs and policing, seem to improve. At the same time, sudden improvement, even if beneficial, can also be insulting. "I don't like it that it takes White people moving into the neighborhood to legitimize our concerns," a long-time resident of a changing neighborhood told Freeman. Years of discrimination and institutional racism, Freeman says, have seared a mistrust of White people and White institutions into the collective memory of Black Americans. (4)

Robin Lester Kenton, who is White, told me she encountered this resentment when she moved to Bedford-Stuyvesant in 2010. She wanted to be a good neighbor and a productive member of the community, so, when neighbors complained of cars speeding down their street, she helped arrange for the Department of Transportation to install a speed bump. She was surprised and hurt when someone said: "They put in a speed bump because you are a White person." She told me she hadn't pulled strings to get a speed bump installed, but, because she had once worked for the Department of Transportation, she knew the complicated procedures necessary to request one—and was successful.

Bruised feelings over the installation of a speed bump were mild compared to the struggles over schools that would ensue as White residents moved into historically Black neighborhoods.

Public schools are anchors in a community. They embody the hopes and dreams for the future, not only among parents whose children are enrolled but also among everyone who lives in a community. They are a second home for many children, a source of comfort and stability. And, in changing neighborhoods, debates around the public schools stir up very strong emotions. (5)

Schools are just about the last thing to change in a gentrifying neighborhood, after the houses have been fixed up, the bike lanes installed, and the fancy restaurants have opened. The first gentrifiers tend to be childless, and, when higher-income families (both White and Black) move in, they tend to take advantage of school choice to avoid struggling schools.

However, by 2015, many of the schools favored by middle-class parents in Brooklyn's gentrified neighborhoods were no longer accepting children from outside their attendance zones—and some didn't even have space for children within their zones. The city's attempt to ease overcrowding at one popular school by redrawing the attendance zone sparked a racially charged conflict.

Angry debates erupted at public hearings over a proposal to shrink the attendance zone for PS 8, a seriously overcrowded, majority-White school in Brooklyn Heights, one of the city's most expensive neighborhoods. The plan called for increasing the attendance zone for PS 307, a mostly Black and Latino school with plenty of room in nearby Vinegar Hill, a neighborhood with a large public housing development called Farragut Houses.

It was, unfortunately, predictable that White parents would object to zone changes that would assign their children to PS 307, a high-poverty school that, despite a warm culture and many enrichment programs, had low test scores. More surprising, at least to me, was the opposition by Black parents who feared the zoning change augured a White takeover of a beloved African American institution.

PS 307 had long been known as a school that serves Black children well. Mama Fela had sent her children to PS 307 in the 1980s, choosing it over local schools in Bedford-Stuyvesant. *New York Times* reporter Nikole Hannah-Jones, who lived in District 16, also enrolled her daughter at PS 307—a choice she wrote about in the *Times* magazine. Now, Black parents were worried that their children would be pushed aside as more White children enrolled. They packed public meetings to voice their opposition to the changes.

"We fought hard to build this school, and we're not just going to let people come from outside when we worked so hard and dedicated ourselves," one mother told *The New York Times.* (6)

The zoning change was ultimately approved. The school's White population grew only modestly after the zone change. Black and Latino children were not displaced; they still made up 80% of PS 307's enrollment in 2022. There was plenty of room for anyone who wanted to attend. But the controversy was a sign of the conflict that gentrification can spark.

Shaila, the *Times* reporter and one the founders of the Bed-Stuy Parents Committee, and Robin, who helped install the speed bump, had no way of knowing that something as seemingly benign as enrolling their children in a local school would stir up strong emotions.

Shaila's plans started innocently enough. While most parents in District 16 sent their children to schools outside the district, Shaila reasoned parents would prefer to keep them close to home. She thought organizing parents of babies and toddlers—before they reached school age—would be a way to build support for the local schools.

She put up flyers in laundromats and on telephone poles. She built an email list and organized meetings. Her new group met on playgrounds and in community centers and encouraged parents to band together and enroll their children in local public schools.

They ran into trouble right away. The official, elected parent body for the district, called the Community Educational Council (CEC), saw this informal group as a rival source of parent power. NeQuan McLean, president of the CEC, said the Bed-Stuy Parents Committee "tried to start a choir" without "speaking to the pastor"—that is, without speaking to him. Even though the CEC and the Bed-Stuy Parents ostensibly had the same goal—building support for the local schools—and even after the newcomers met with McLean, he resented the fact that they had begun organizing without first seeking his permission. Friction between the CEC and the Bed-Stuy Parents Committee would keep the two groups from working together effectively, leading to turf battles that blocked any progress.

"They felt we were stepping on their territory," Shana Cooper-Silas, a Black mother in the Bed-Stuy Parents Committee, told me a few years later over drinks after work one night. "It was perceived as an all-White group that was trying to change schools for White people."

The Bed-Stuy Parents Committee ran into further difficulties in early 2016. The group reasoned that parents would be more willing to enroll their children if the schools allowed prospective parents to visit. But while charter schools had organized tours for prospective parents, most of the ordinary public schools saw no need to market themselves, even as their enrollments plummeted.

Two schools did offer tours for prospective parents: Brighter Choice and another school a mile away, PS 309. (Brighter Choice had even hired a public relations firm to help create a "brand" for the school and market it to new parents.)

"Those two schools had coffee and donuts for us," Shana said. When they called other schools and asked for a tour, Shana said, the response was "Huh? You want to do what?'"

The Bed-Stuy Parents Committee ran into a reality that surprised them—and that helps explain at least one reason why schools in gentrifying neighborhoods remain economically and racially segregated: Some high-poverty schools, actively or inadvertently, discourage middle-class families from enrolling. The schools may be too overwhelmed by day-to-day operations to schedule tours—or to respond to phone calls from prospective parents. But some school administrators are also wary of the sense of entitlement that middle-class parents bring; they see these parents, particularly White parents, as pushy, imperious, and a challenge to their authority. Low-income families, because of their work schedules, are less likely to make demands and are less likely to be around during the day to complain.

"In some schools, the principal doesn't want a strong PTA," Andrew Marshall, an African American parent leader at PS 282, a Brooklyn school in neighboring District 13 that welcomes parent involvement, told me. "They don't want parents in the building asking 'Why don't the bathrooms have toilet paper or soap? Why are the teachers yelling at the children?'" (7)

Almost by default, the Bed-Stuy Parents Committee picked Brighter Choice and PS 309 as the places they would enroll their children. The two schools seemed like welcoming places, and, in the fall of 2016, these families enrolled 14 children in prekindergarten: 6 at Brighter Choice, and 8 at PS 309.

The newcomers at PS 309 put their organizing skills to work. They held a book sale. They arranged for low-cost music lessons. They staged a mock election on election day. One mother made plans to spruce up the playground and school garden.

Robin used her connections with the Department of Transportation to set up a fundraising event called Touch-a-Truck, arranging for the city to loan the school 15 bulldozers, garbage trucks, and other large vehicles. Parents bought inexpensive tickets and children were able to climb on the trucks and honk the horns on the playground. Someone brought pumpkins for the children to paint. The event brought in $2,000—more than the PTA had ever raised.

But there was friction almost from the start. Seven of the children of the Bed-Stuy Parents Committee members were White—the only White children in the school; one was biracial (with a White mother). Six were placed in one prekindergarten class, and just two assigned to the other prekindergarten class. Rumors spread that the White parents had asked for an all-White class—rumors that the White parents denied but that circulated for months.

"There was no trust between anyone," Robin told me.

Some of the parents who had been at the school for years resented the fact that the newcomers called themselves the Bed-Stuy Parents Committee, that they were appropriating a name that was synonymous with Black Brooklyn for a group that seemed to represent a White takeover of the neighborhood. The PTA president, Natasha Seaton, who was at the school all day every day, felt the newcomers talked down to her.

"They have their nice prestigious jobs," the PTA president, known as Miss Tasha, told the School Colors podcast. "You're talking to me like, oh you're higher than me." (8) When Shaila sent emails using her *New York Times* address, it seemed she was flaunting her status. "Don't you have a Gmail account?" another mother asked. "Are you doing that, even if not on purpose, to be intimidating?"

The newcomers complained that the PTA failed to follow the chancellor's regulations on everything from financial record-keeping to advance notice of meetings. The newcomers resented the fact that a security guard scowled at them and required them to sign in at the front desk—when Miss Tasha could walk into the school without signing in.

Several White mothers lobbied to be allowed to drop their 4-year-olds off in the classroom, rather than in the cafeteria. Very small children, they said, had trouble separating from their parents. The quiet of their classroom was less stressful than the bustle of the cafeteria. Their request was eventually granted, but some felt it was another example of entitled parents throwing their weight around. Miss Tasha even accused the White parents of wanting an all-White school; the White parents felt that their efforts on behalf of the school were unwelcome.

Parents quarreled among themselves. Teachers and parents were at odds with one another. And there was friction between the principal and the staff, parents and teachers told me.

"The defense mechanism is finger-pointing," said Robin. While the newcomers were trying to help, she said, their efforts were seen as sneaky and undercutting the current PTA. "It was crazy. It's hard to be a part of it, but it's hard to rise above. A lot of us, including myself, were naïve about what was going on."

Unspoken was the anger over changes in the neighborhood that left long-time parents feeling marginalized—and fearful about any changes in the school. Significantly, Miss Tasha had moved from Bedford-Stuyvesant to Staten Island some time before; she continued to travel from Staten Island to PS 309 each day with her child. She felt she had been forced out of the neighborhood, and she didn't want to be also forced out of the school.

Among the newcomers, Robin, vice-president for marketing at the Brooklyn Public Library, had enrolled her son at PS 309 thinking her marketing and fundraising skills would be welcomed. "There are PTAs that raise a million dollars, and they get to keep that money," she said. "These parents don't have the time or the skills to do that, and this is criminal that they are underfunded. I thought, 'We should be there to help support them with resources.' I was just not thinking about the emotional impact of all of us being like, 'We're here!'"

After the first year, half of the parents from the Bed-Stuy Parents Committee withdrew their children from PS 309. After the second year, all of them had left. The school's enrollment steadily declined, from 500 in 2006 to 237 in 2016, to 204 in 2017. By 2021, it had dropped to 171. PS 309, like many other District 16 schools, was caught in a downward spiral. The newcomers had failed to reverse the declining enrollment at PS 309, and the possibility of building a school where White and Black children could learn together seemed ever more remote. As Mama Fela suggested, there was just too much bitterness and anger.

Compared to the conflicts at PS 309, the arrival of newcomers at Brighter Choice was mostly harmonious. The children who entered Brighter Choice with the Bed-Stuy Parents Committee included both Black and White pupils—unlike PS 309 where they were nearly all White. Ms. Fabayo, confident in her own leadership, welcomed the newcomers.

"I was never intimidated by New Brooklyn, as I will call it," she said. "I was never intimidated by a savvier parent. I liked it." And, unlike the principal at PS 309, Ms. Fabayo would step in whenever there were disagreements among parents, mediating before little problems turned into big ones.

But Brighter Choice would encounter other issues that would threaten its continued success. In early 2016, the city Department of Education, in line with one of de Blasio's school improvement strategies, decided to merge Brighter Choice and Young Scholars, another school in the same building. If an effective school like Brighter Choice absorbs a less successful one, the thinking went, students may benefit from the leadership in the stronger school. Moreover, mergers save money: Because fixed costs are high—each school needs a principal and core administrative staff—it's expensive to have very small schools sharing a building. Tiny schools may not have the resources to offer special education services or programs such as music and art. So, in the fall of 2016, Brighter Choice absorbed Young Scholars. Overnight, enrollment doubled, as did the staff. (The other school in the building, for disabled children, would continue with its own principal and staff.) The population of Brighter Choice changed: In 2008, it had only a few homeless children. After the 2016 merger, there were dozens of children in temporary housing. "They bring in issues that break your heart," Ms. Fabayo told InsideSchools.

The merger brought other challenges. If Ms. Fabayo's task in 2008 had been to find parents willing to take a chance on her new school, her challenge in 2016 would be to bring into the fold parents and staff who had *not* chosen Brighter Choice. Parents and teachers from Young Scholars had different experiences and different expectations from those at Brighter Choice.

"A merger is like a prearranged marriage where two folks are getting together and you hope it works out," Ms. Fabayo told me. While she understood the rationale for combining the schools, there were inevitable culture clashes. "Everyone is hurt in a merger because everyone loses something," she said. "They called it a merger, but Young Scholars was closed. In a sense, Brighter Choice closed, too."

In the fall of 2016, even as the enrollment doubled, Ms. Fabayo continued to greet every child by name. The school still had interdisciplinary social studies projects—such as the 2nd-graders' transportation study that included trips to the train show at the New York Botanical Garden and the Transit Museum. Math lessons still combined hands-on work with skill drills; class trips were frequent.

But it was hard to bridge the culture gap between the schools. Brighter Choice had a more progressive approach, with "center time" where small children could choose an activity and move around the classroom. The school was part of a city program called PROSE, in which teachers agree to be flexible about contract rules in exchange for more say in the curriculum. Young Scholars teachers, many of whom had taught at the old PS 304, had to adapt to a new school culture and, understandably, some were resentful. Instead of being one big happy family, there was friction.

Meanwhile, Shana, the African American mother from the Bed-Stuy Parents Committee who had enrolled her child in prekindergarten, threw herself into volunteer work. As PTA president, she helped organize a "gala" that raised more than $10,000—an unheard-of sum for the school. Together with Ms. Fabayo, the PTA set up an after-school program for prekindergartners called BCCS Enrich. Brighter Choice had long offered a free after-school program, paid with regular school funds, for children starting in kindergarten, but the new program served younger children. Parents paid a monthly fee to the PTA, which ran the program.

Shana's daughter had a good year for prekindergarten, but the 2017–2018 school year was difficult. The kindergarten teacher, hired at the last minute, couldn't control the classroom, and the children were unruly. Ms. Fabayo told me she realized almost immediately that she'd made a mistake hiring the teacher and had her removed within a few months. However, she was unable to find a replacement midyear. Recruiting qualified teachers to high-poverty schools is always difficult. Many teachers prefer schools in high-income neighborhoods where they believe the working conditions are easier. And, if finding a qualified teacher to start in September is difficult, finding one to begin midyear is next to impossible. So, from January until June, the class had a rotating group of substitutes and teachers' aides, called paraprofessionals. By late winter, Shana began looking for alternatives. She entered a lottery for a charter school a few miles away. When her daughter was admitted, she left Brighter Choice.

After 10 years at Brighter Choice, Ms. Fabayo was also ready to leave. When she was offered a promotion to a job at the Department of Education headquarters in downtown Manhattan, she jumped at the chance. (She would later return to District 16 as deputy superintendent, and then leave the city for an administrative job near her home in Valley Stream, a Long Island suburb.)

Ms. Fabayo had been working to build a school that honored African American culture and history while welcoming children of other backgrounds; one that offered low-income children a creative, progressive curriculum that's common in wealthier neighborhoods. But schools like Brighter Choice are fragile. Even one disappointing teacher can hurt a school's reputation. More important, the loss of the visionary founding principal, combined with the disruption of the merger, dealt the school a blow from which it would be hard to recover.

In June 2018, parents at Brighter Choice learned that they had a new principal: Jeremy Daniel. For many, he seemed like an odd choice: He had an impressive resume, having studied at Harvard School of Education and Columbia University's Teachers College. A former Peace Corp volunteer in Morocco, he spoke Spanish, French, and Arabic. But all his teaching and administrative work had been at middle and high schools in Manhattan; he had never taught elementary school. And, in a school in a Black neighborhood that was undergoing gentrification, the fact that he was White and lived outside the neighborhood rubbed some people the wrong way. For parents who remembered a time when school leaders were almost always White, the appointment seemed like a step backward to a less equitable time. Some worried the school would lose its role as a community institution that gave Black children pride in their heritage. Others worried that Mr. Daniel's lack of elementary school experience might stall the school's progress implementing progressive teaching techniques.

When the announcement came down that Mr. Daniel was the new principal, parents requested a meeting with Rahesha Amon-Harrison, the superintendent of their school district, District 16, to explain how he had been chosen. She agreed to a meeting a few weeks later. About 60 parents waited in the auditorium that night, but when the superintendent arrived, she refused to speak to the parents and left without any explanation—saying only that she was unprepared. Parents were angry and confused. (9)

Parents never got a clear explanation, but typically principals of high-poverty schools are drawn from a very small pool of candidates. Many potential candidates prefer low-poverty schools where they believe it's easier to produce successful results. While some excellent principals, motivated by a sense of social justice, choose to lead high-poverty schools, there aren't enough experienced and effective administrators to fill all vacancies.

According to the chancellor's regulations, a district superintendent in New York City may appoint an "interim acting principal" to fill a vacancy without consulting the school community, as Ms. Amon-Harrison did with Mr. Daniel. A committee of parents and teachers, called a C-30 committee, is then supposed to interview candidates before the appointment is made official. In Mr. Daniel's case, the C-30 committee did eventually interview candidates; Mr. Daniel, despite his lack of elementary school experience, was far and away the most qualified, Lauren Harris, a parent on the committee told me. (Lauren told me later, it was "surreal" how *unqualified* the other candidates were.) But the clumsy rollout of the announcement and the superintendent's refusal to talk about how she made the decision left bad feelings.

When school began in September 2018, Mr. Daniel was on his own to win over the community. By all accounts he tried hard. Although it was an hour and a half commute from his home in Upper Manhattan, he was at the school by 7:00 A.M. every day and rarely left before 5:00 P.M. On Saturdays, he even came in for "skate club" to skateboard with kids on the playground.

"He's super receptive, good at building trust with the staff, super-generous with parents," said Virginia Poundstone, an artist, a White mother, and a member of the Bed-Stuy Parents Committee who enrolled her son in prekindergarten that fall. "But it wasn't without hiccups for sure. He was replacing a beloved, founding principal who was from the neighborhood."

Enrollment was creeping up, to 319 from 303 the year before. The school opened two classes for 3-year-olds, called "3K," as part of de Blasio's campaign to expand free early childhood education. The number of White pupils nearly doubled, from 12 to 22, almost all in the youngest grades. The school was attracting more middle-class families as well: The proportion of children poor enough to qualify for free lunch dropped to 80% from 85% the year before.

The school had lost Shana as PTA president. The new PTA president, CeCe Everett, also Black, was apprehensive about the changes she saw at the school. "We don't need the change makers right now," she told the podcast School Colors. (10) Other parents told me she was openly hostile to Mr. Daniel and took out her resentment in petty ways, such as holding meetings without informing him.

Some debates in the PTA fell on racial and class lines. Many Black parents were put off (and many White parents were embarrassed) by the attitude of at least one White father who seemed to embody the sense of entitlement that made long-time residents suspicious of newcomers. At every opportunity, this father lobbied for children to go outside for recess on cold days (rather than watch videos in the auditorium) with an insistence that began to wear even on those parents who basically agreed with him. He buttonholed other parents and staff, presented scholarly research showing the importance of outdoor play, and complained over and over again as if watching videos at recess was the most pressing problem the school faced. Many Black and Latino parents, fearful the cold weather would trigger asthma attacks and worried that their children didn't have warm enough winter coats, were wary of sending their children out in the cold. It was irritating to have a White man insist that they should.

But a more serious conflict emerged when the PTA treasurer, Talia Braude, who is White, discovered $7,000 was missing from the PTA account for the after-school program for 3- and 4-year-olds. Parents had been paying the PTA about $200 a month for after-school. The PTA had been paying the after-school staff out of that account.

Without informing Talia, CeCe had told parents to make payments to a new online portal, not directly to the PTA. The new account was in CeCe's name, not the PTA's. Talia emailed CeCe to ask what was going on and when she received no reply, she informed Mr. Daniel and the assistant principal, LaTrace Finney, who told her to contact the central Department of Education to report a possible case of embezzlement. The official in central told her to contact the police.

"Going to the police to report a Black woman would not have been my first port of call but I was told I had to," Talia told me later. "And I walked around with this feeling that half of the school was like, 'What is this White woman doing reporting one of our people to the police?' and the other half is going 'Why did this treasurer lose $7,000 of ours?' So, it was really ugly and miserable."

It was understandable that CeCe, who was unemployed and volunteering at the school 40 hours a week, would want to get paid for her work. To do that in line with the chancellor's regulations, however, she would have had to follow certain procedures to be approved as a vendor. Instead, she simply told parents to stop paying the PTA and to pay her instead—leaving the PTA without the $7,000 it needed to pay the after-school staff.

"You know, it's not set up in a fair way," Talia said. "Rich parents [in other schools] can spend 40 hours a week on the PTA because they have a trust fund or a partner who earns $500,000 a year, but CeCe who is doing a lot of great things for the PTA was still struggling to feed her kids. I'm sorry that sucks, but the solution is not to take $7,000 from the PTA." (CeCe didn't respond to texts or phone messages I sent asking to speak to her.)

Talia felt let down by the school administration, which she felt wanted to wash its hands of the problem. The police told her to make a report to the District Attorney; she never heard what became of her complaint.

CeCe took her children out of school. Lauren, the PTA secretary, became interim PTA president. Talia and Lauren managed to straighten out the books, canceling some contracts and stretching the money they had left to keep the after-school program going until the end of the year. They had help from Frances, the PTA vice president and a billing specialist for a large law firm. When Keesha, whose son was in 1st grade, agreed to join the PTA, they were glad for the extra help.

Meanwhile, a few other parents, both Black and White, were becoming disenchanted with the school. For Virginia's son, prekindergarten was a rocky year. He was an active 4-year-old, and there seemed to be too much time spent sitting down. Like all the classrooms at Brighter Choice, his class had a SmartBoard—an electronic screen that serves as both a blackboard and a projector for images from the Internet.

"There was way too much YouTube watching, so much TV watching," she said. "They didn't go outside in the winter. His behavior became horrendous. He was no longer helpful at home. He screamed a lot more." Mr. Daniel would make it a priority to incorporate movement into children's days—with more outdoor recess and opportunities to move indoors—but it would come too late for Virginia's son.

By winter, Virginia was looking for alternatives. She entered a lottery for a racially mixed charter school with a substantial number of middle-class families about 2 miles away. Her son won a spot and he enrolled. About half of her son's prekindergarten class—mostly families who had been part of the Bed-Stuy Parents Committee—left Brighter Choice in June 2019. There were 13 White children in the two pre-K classes in 2018–2019; the following year there were just 3 White children in kindergarten.

This is a pattern in many schools in changing neighborhoods: Middle-class White parents take advantage of the city's free prekindergarten classes, then transfer their children to private schools or public schools that have more middle-class children. This can cause resentment, disappointment, and hurt feelings among the staff, as well as among the parents who stay. "I guess we're not good enough for them," one teacher told me after the White children withdrew in 2019.

Talia and Lauren kept their children in the school for 1st grade. They agreed to continue their work in the PTA, Talia as treasurer and Lauren as recording secretary.

"You don't walk away from a school because you have one bad year," Talia told me later. "I stayed on for another year because everybody asked me to. Nobody else wanted to be the treasurer. And so, I stuck it out."

Talia, who learned about Brighter Choice through the Bed-Stuy Parents Committee, had picked the school in the hopes that she and her son, Rian, would make friends across racial lines—something she had missed as a child in South Africa where she attended an all-White, Jewish day school.

"I grew up with so many racial and religious stereotypes that I'm still trying to shake," she told me over coffee after she dropped Rian off at school one morning. Talia didn't mind that Rian was one of the few White children in the school, as long as he felt he belonged. "I want him to understand other cultures," she said. "I'm happy to have him be in the minority."

As a single mother, she enjoyed the camaraderie of the parents at Brighter Choice. An architect in private practice, she had bought and renovated a three-family house in the neighborhood and rented the top floor to Lauren, another single mother.

Lauren, who works as an occupational therapist in a public middle school in another Brooklyn neighborhood, had felt uneasy serving as interim PTA president. As a White woman, she knew wasn't representative of most parents at the school and she preferred to serve in a supporting role. "I'm not going to try to change everything, I don't think that's my place," said Lauren. "I just want to be part of the community."

Both Talia and Lauren were relieved when Keesha agreed to step up to a leadership role in the PTA.

In June 2019, Keesha was elected PTA president, unopposed. She had a daunting to-do list: She had to reestablish trust in the PTA after the scandal of the missing money. She had to mediate the dispute over recess. She had to manage parents' fears that gentrification was taking over their neighborhood—and their school. Ever optimistic, she was eager to put the troubles of the spring behind them and start afresh in the fall.

SIX

Bringing the Community Together

courtesy of InsideSchools.org

Can the school keep its focus on Black culture while making room for children of other races?

Just a week after the first day of school in 2019, three dozen mothers and fathers—the majority of them Black, but also a few White and Latino—gathered in the early evening in the sweltering school auditorium for the first PTA meeting of the year. A noisy fan droned in the back, making it hard to hear. The audience, in hard wooden seats bolted to the floor, fanned themselves with their programs.

Standing on the stage with a handheld microphone, Keesha's most pressing task was to build trust among the parents after the racially charged quarrels and the allegations of embezzlement of PTA funds the previous year. She introduced herself and the other members of the PTA executive board: all mothers, five Black, three White, each with formidable talents and resumes—a lawyer, an architect, an actor, a speech therapist, an occupational therapist, a billing specialist for a large law firm, the owner of a catering business, and Keesha, a customer service representative for Verizon.

Keesha explained they were all volunteers—not paid employees, as some parents mistakenly thought—and their mission was to serve all parents and make sure all voices were heard. Then Mr. Daniel, the principal, rose to report on initiatives for the year: new reading textbooks, a new social studies curriculum called "Civics for All"; science discovery kits; the school garden; the newly hired "play coaches" assigned to the playground at recess.

Keesha asked if parents had questions.

A Black mother raised her hand to be recognized.

"The principal who founded the school promoted African culture and principles. With the new principal, what direction is the school going to take? Is it going to be different?" she asked.

The woman said aloud what many had been thinking. Brighter Choice had been founded on the model of an Afrocentric nursery school called Little Sun People, a haven for Black children in the neighborhood. Many parents in the room had sent their children to Little Sun People; they chose Brighter Choice because they thought it would be a continuation of that kind of education.

Brighter Choice has long had a rich arts program, called Ifetayo, which offers African dance, drumming, and arts with the goal of building a strong cultural identity among children of African descent. The school has long taken pride in the way it teaches African American history and culture. Black History Month was not just a time for obligatory odes to Martin Luther King, but a chance to study in-depth Black activists like W. E. B. Du Bois, Medgar Evers, Malcolm X, and Marcus Garvey.

But the school was changing, with increasing numbers of Latino children and, more recently, White children. With a White principal, and with changing demographics, what was the future of the school?

Without missing a beat, Keesha responded with her vision for the school community. "We're not going to lose our foundation, but we are going to build on it to include other cultures," she said. "We want the school to be a family. African people, Spanish people, whoever is here. We don't want anyone to feel they are not heard; they are not seen."

Another mother in the audience, Lurie Daniel Favors, echoed the first mother's concern. "Gentrification is real," said Lurie, a civil rights lawyer and chair of the School Leadership Team (SLT), a body of parents, teachers, and administrators—separate from the PTA—that is charged with developing policy for the school. "White nationalism is also real. There is a lot of concern," she added. "We're not operating solely in a Black–White paradigm. What do we do for Spanish-speaking children? What do we do for Spanish-speaking children with African ancestry? What about multiracial families?"

Keesha replied. "It's good to discuss this, so long as the parent body is open to conversations. I ask all of you who are concerned to come to the School Leadership Team meetings."

A father raised his hand to be recognized. "It's 2020 and still no air-conditioning!"

The lack of air-conditioning is just one example of the inequalities in a school system that offers better resources to children in wealthy neighborhoods than in low-income ones. As Keesha would discover, the school had problems that were outside her control, and air-conditioning was one of them. For now, the PTA would serve as a forum to share concerns and to spur the school administration to do what it could within its own limitations—a first step toward solving the problem.

The father who complained may have known intuitively what researchers have confirmed: Air-conditioning is important not just for children's comfort, but also for their academic achievement. Teachers know that children have trouble concentrating when classrooms are hot. Scientists know that when bodies overheat, they sweat to cool off. That reduces blood circulation to the brain—and brain function.

A team of scholars from the National Bureau of Economic Research, based on data from millions of students, has found that children do worse on standardized tests in years when there are more days above 80 degrees, a problem that is exacerbated by climate change. Air-conditioning mitigates the impact significantly. (1)

But many schools, particularly those serving primarily Black and Latino children, don't have air-conditioning. Some public schools in wealthy neighborhoods, such as PS 6 on the Upper East Side and PS 87 on the Upper West Side of Manhattan, pay for air-conditioning with PTA funds—money raised by parents. Schools in Bedford-Stuyvesant, with lower-income families, usually can't do that. And even if they find the money for air-conditioning units, they sometimes can't install them. Parents at PS 262 in Bedford-Stuyvesant secured donations for air-conditioning, but the building's wiring was too old to support it. (2)

Not only are the schools in Black and Latino neighborhoods less likely to have air-conditioning, but these neighborhoods also tend to be hotter. That's a legacy of redlining in the 1930s, when the federal government denied mortgage guarantees to Black neighborhoods, considering them a credit risk. A recent study by researchers at the University of Richmond found formerly redlined neighborhoods were, on average, 5 degrees hotter; they had fewer trees and parks and more paved areas, such as highways, that absorb heat. (3)

The New York City Health Department ranks neighborhoods according to how vulnerable residents are to injury or death due to the heat. Neighborhoods with the fewest trees and the most asphalt have a high "heat vulnerability index." Bedford-Stuyvesant is one of the neighborhoods with the highest level of heat vulnerability in the city. (4)

In 2017, when about one quarter of the city's classrooms lacked air-conditioning, Mayor Bill de Blasio vowed that the city would install units in all classrooms by 2022 (although not in common spaces like gyms and cafeterias). (5) That promise was small comfort to the parents at Brighter Choice on a hot September night.

Mr. Daniel rose to respond to the father's query. He told the PTA he had filed a request for air-conditioning with the district office the year before. He had never received a reply. He promised to keep working on the issue.

Even if the PTA couldn't bring air-conditioning to Brighter Choice, it could do a lot to create a sense of common purpose among parents and children in the school. The Saturday after the PTA meeting, the PTA organized its first community-building activity in Prospect Park, the 500-acre landscape designed by Frederick Law Olmstead and Calvert Vaux about 4 miles from Brighter Choice.

Keesha and her husband Keyonn laid out baked goods, brought by other parents, on folding tables just outside the historic Carousel, a charming attraction that the PTA had rented for 2 hours for $500. Their son Keyonn, in 2nd grade, greeted his friends; the children rode the carved wooden horses as many times as they liked while parents chatted with one another and purchased cookies, cakes, and juice. It was a chance for returning parents and those who were new to the school to get to know one another in a relaxed way.

The following Tuesday, Fathers on a Mission, the fathers' group at Brighter Choice, organized "Dads, Take Your Child to School Day." Breakfast was laid out on folding tables in the lobby outside the auditorium. Fathers posed for photos with their children, grinning broadly through cardboard frames tagged "We love BCCS," as Brighter Choice Community School is known.

Every Saturday morning, parents and children came to the school for "skate club," organized by the principal. Children could learn to ride skateboards and parents, especially fathers, had a chance to chat with one another. To join them, Mr. Daniel rode the subway from his home in Northern Manhattan. On one Saturday, Mr. Daniel set up a grill, fried eggs, and offered egg sandwiches to parents and children.

The biggest and most popular event was the Fall Festival on a Saturday in mid-October, a day of activities that included a Double Dutch competition and a yard sale with toys, books, clothes, and housewares. Talia created a "junkyard playground"—where kids could make their own creations from cardboard boxes, cardboard tubes, and tape. Mr. Daniel read picture books aloud in Spanish to one group of children. Dads flipped burgers on the barbecue. Kids made fruit smoothies with a contraption that used a stationary bicycle to power a blender—so that peddling the bike would make the blender spin. The weather was delightfully warm and sunny, and everyone seemed to enjoy the day.

The debate over recess—begun by the insistent White father the year before—continued that fall. Keesha was ambivalent: Her son, Keyonn, had asthma, and cold weather sometimes triggered attacks. In fact, he had spent one Christmas Eve in the emergency room—an episode she didn't want to repeat. At the same time, she agreed with parents who thought children would benefit from more exercise—especially if it could be done safely.

The school administration brokered a compromise: Children would go out if it wasn't raining or frigid; the school, with the help of the PTA, would collect extra hats, gloves, scarves, and coats to make sure everyone was warmly dressed. A few parents who had insisted that children go out to play, even in the rain, were disappointed, but most parents seemed satisfied.

Then, at the November PTA meeting, there were more complaints. Mr. Daniel, it seems, had sent children out to play on a day that some parents thought was too cold. Parents peppered Mr. Daniel with questions about his decision. At what point is it too cold to go out? What about children with health problems?

Mr. Daniel apologized. "I made a bad decision a few weeks ago," he said. "It was sunny but cold."

Keesha intervened, once again suggesting that disagreements were best resolved by open discussions. "Come out and have these discussions so we can make a decision with everyone's input," she said. The discussions would continue at the monthly meetings of the School Leadership Team.

If the PTA had very limited formal power, the School Leadership Team was a place where discussions could, in fact, lead to concrete changes. Parent Teacher Associations, in New York City and elsewhere, plan activities, raise money for special projects, and serve as an advocate for parents. In New York City, however, each school also has a School Leadership Team (SLT) and this body—made up of parents, teachers, and administrators—has the authority to set educational priorities and shape the direction of the school. The formal role of the SLT is to draw up an annual "comprehensive education plan" with goals for the school; the principal is charged with developing a budget in line with those goals. At Brighter Choice, the SLT's monthly meetings became the place where parents hashed out their grievances about the school—and administrators, teachers, and parents worked together to find solutions.

The SLT met in the early evening in an empty classroom and usually drew a few dozen parents, as well as Mr. Daniel and a few teachers. Lurie, the African American civil rights lawyer who had raised concerns at the first PTA meeting about the impact of gentrification, began the October SLT meeting with the suggestion that the school was paying inadequate attention to Hispanic Heritage Month, the mid-September to mid-October annual celebration of Latino contributions to U.S. history and culture. While some 30% of the children at Brighter Choice were Latino, their culture was not well represented at the school, she said, and Spanish-speaking parents rarely attended PTA or SLT meetings.

The conversation shifted to complaints about the school's dual language program, designed to make children fluent in both Spanish and English. The program, introduced several years before, was one of the school's main selling points, and many of the middle-class parents had chosen Brighter Choice for its promise to teach their children in two languages. But a dozen parents at the meeting said their children were hardly learning any Spanish. One mother pointed out that there weren't even labels in Spanish in the classrooms. Another said that after 2 years in school, her child couldn't even say "*ti amo*."

Mr. Daniel, who speaks Spanish, agreed that the school needed to make a concerted effort to make Spanish-speaking parents feel welcome at school meetings. He pointed to the Saturday skate club as a successful activity that brought in a range of families. And he promised to organize a "dual language symposium," or open house, so parents could visit their children's classrooms during the day and observe how Spanish was taught.

Ms. Deittra, the staff member who served as "parent coordinator," or liaison between the administration and parents, took responsibility for making sure that all the signs and labels in the school were in both English and Spanish—a way to make Spanish-speaking parents feel welcome while also exposing children in the dual-language classes to more written Spanish. She sent out text messages and emails to parents in both English and Spanish.

As the year went on, there would be a few signs of discord between Black and Latino parents and staff. For example, at least one Latino family felt slighted when the Black security guard checked their IDs when they entered the school but allowed Black parents to come in without showing IDs. One Black parent complained of a racist slight by a Dominican teacher. Spanish-speaking parents who tried to participate in school events occasionally felt left out—one Spanish-speaking parent left a meeting I attended because there was no one available to translate for her—but the school was making an effort to better integrate the Spanish-speaking members of the community. In the main, the school seemed like a happy place.

The autumn's activities, especially the Carousel and the Fall Festival, had built a sense of belonging. The forums to air grievances—the PTA and the SLT—gave parents a sense they were being heard. Keesha was proud of the progress she had made bringing the school community together. But she was worn out juggling the demands of work, her responsibilities at home, and her role as PTA president.

"I have lofty ideas and aspirations and—What are we in, October?" she said one morning as I rode with her to her office in Downtown Brooklyn. "Oh, wow. How many more months of this?"

There were endless meetings, it seemed, not just the monthly PTA and SLT meetings, but executive board meetings and meetings with other PTA presidents and community organizations. And there were near constant emails from parents and school officials.

"I just got an email yesterday that says I have to facilitate a Title 1 meeting"—a parents' committee that allocates federal money given to high poverty schools under Title 1 of the Elementary and Secondary Education Act—"and I'm looking at these emails like 'Oh, wow.' No clue, no clue about some of these things."

The PTA job was much more demanding than she had anticipated. Her paid job required attention—she couldn't interrupt work to deal with PTA business during the day. The emails from other parents were driving her crazy. Her husband was cranky about the amount of time she spent on PTA business.

"I don't stop. I wake up," she said. "There are emails that start before I even look at my phone. By 9 o'clock, I probably have five threads that are already in progress, and they don't stop throughout the day."

When she picks up Little Keyonn each day from the after-school program around 5:00 P.M., she takes care of business in the PTA office, distributing T-shirts, arranging "picture day," or reminding people about meetings.

"I get home after six, close to seven. I have to cook dinner, and it starts all over," she said.

To make matters worse, Keesha has a heart disease called hypertrophic cardiomyopathy, a condition that seems to be more prevalent in the African American community. She gets chest pains and gets so lightheaded that she's on the verge of passing out. "Just out of nowhere my heart would race like I was running a marathon," she said.

Keesha also has asthma, high blood pressure, and high cholesterol, conditions that are more prevalent among African Americans, even controlling for income and education. A public health researcher, Arline Geronimus, says the cumulative effect of dealing with the stress of racism produces what she calls "weathering," or premature aging, especially among Black women. Hypertrophic cardiomyopathy, a disease associated with aging, is more likely to hurt Black women in midlife, Geronimus told me. (6) Whatever the cause, racialized health disparities are a fact of life for Keesha.

Talia, too, was tired. She and Lauren were organizing a candy sale to raise money for a 5th-grade class trip to Frost Valley, a YMCA camp an hour north of the city. If every child in the school sold a few boxes of candy, the proceeds could pay for an overnight trip to the environmental education center where children would learn about nature and take part in team-building activities. It seemed like a simple enough project. But keeping track of all the orders and making sure the children paid for the candy they took was proving to be a complicated task—"months of misery," she told me later. And she had to deal with complaints from the PTA's "wellness committee"—parents who wanted a healthy alternative to candy.

Still, the PTA finances seemed to be in order. Talia's detailed monthly reports and Keesha's transparency had restored trust in the PTA after the turmoil of the previous year.

Talia and Lauren had taken on responsibility for setting up Family Movie Night, a monthly Friday activity organized by the PTA and Fathers on a Mission. They showed movies like *Coco, Inside Out, A Wrinkle in Time,* and *Mad Hot Ballroom*. While everyone pitched in, Talia and Lauren, because they had flexible work schedules, were able to get to the school earlier than some other parents to make popcorn, get snacks to sell, set up the movie, and get tickets—admission was $2—so everything was ready by the time people arrived at 5:30 P.M.

And, along with Ms. Deittra, Talia and Lauren were organizing an event called The Gift of Giving. The idea was to collect gently used, good-quality items that parents might like to receive as gifts such as books, candles, neckties, jewelry, and picture frames. These things would be set up in the PTA room, and the children could "shop" for presents for their parents for the holidays. Being active in the PTA was a lot of work.

At the December 12 PTA meeting, Keesha organized a spread of fried chicken wings, Chinese fried rice, pancakes, spring rolls, cold cuts, strawberries, cupcakes, and cookies. Talia gave an update on fundraising for the Frost Valley trip. Keesha summed up the PTA's accomplishments for the year so far: the Carousel, movie nights, the Fall Festival, the candy sale, Friendsgiving (a potluck supper just before Thanksgiving). She invited everyone to the Winter Concert the following week. "It will blow you away," she said. "If you know anything about BCCS, they put on a *show*!"

When she opened the floor to questions and comments, one mother remarked on how much the atmosphere at the school had changed since the year before.

"You guys have turned a lot of things around from last year," this mother said. "You gained the community's trust."

The Winter Concert on the morning of December 18 was well-attended. Spanish-speaking parents who didn't usually come to PTA meetings were there, as well as lots of grandparents. Parents with inflexible jobs managed to take a few hours off. Talia staffed the bake-sale table in the corridor outside the auditorium, selling cookies and cakes and ingenious little kits that she had created to make gingerbread houses. Keesha, wearing a Santa Claus cap, slim black pants, UGG boots, and gold hoop earrings, welcomed parents as they entered. A few dozen parents stood in the back because all the seats were filled. Everyone leaned forward with their cellphones to record videos of the children singing a multi-ethnic, multicultural round of songs recognizing holidays of different faiths.

Two teachers welcomed the parents—alternating between Spanish and English, so that everyone could understand. The smallest children, the 3-year-olds, dressed in red and green, sang Darlene Love's version of "Santa Claus Is Coming to Town." The prekindergartners, all dressed in white and blue, sang, "Hanukkah, Light the Menorah." Kindergartners wearing black and kente cloth sang a Kwanzaa song. First-graders, dressed in white, sang about Ramadan; 2nd-graders sang about Diwali, the Hindu festival of lights; 3rd-graders sang about the Latino holiday of Three Kings Day; 4th-graders sang a song about Junkanoo, a Caribbean festival. Fifth-graders in black pants, white shirts, and red ties played a medley on keyboard, drum, and rhythm instruments.

"Feliz Navidad!" Mr. Daniel proclaimed from the stage after the 5th-graders had finished. "What it comes down to is unity," Mr. Daniel said. "There are divisions right now, nationally, internationally, and in our neighborhoods. Unity is our message." He said the same thing in Spanish. Then he thanked Keesha, who added: "We are stronger together."

Everyone, including the audience, then sang "Feliz Navidad" in Spanish and English, standing, swaying to the music, with kids in the aisles clapping to the beat.

After the concert, I drove with Keesha and her husband Keyonn to her office. She was feeling good. There were no longer factions in the PTA, she said, and there was more interaction among different groups of parents. She felt she was working closely with the principal, and she was pleased with how open he was to feedback. Yes, parents had plenty of concerns—about the lack of air-conditioning, the decision to have recess outdoors in the freezing cold, and the quality of Spanish instruction—but the PTA and the School Leadership Team provided forums to address them.

"After the last PTA meeting [during which parents complained about outdoor recess], I went to Mr. Daniel and I explained to him, 'Listen, these are good problems because we have parents who feel comfortable enough to let us know what's going on.' I'd rather they let us know what is going on than just talk about it among themselves and complain. We welcome the feedback."

"What did you do to bring about unity?" I asked.

"My strategy is very simple," she said. "I was kind. I was open. We are a service to our community. That's what brought the community together."

SEVEN

Problems Outside the School's Control

Kristina Bumphrey/Kristina B. Photography

Mr. Daniel wrestles with chronic absenteeism caused by homelessness.

While Keesha was working to build a sense of community among parents, Mr. Daniel was struggling with issues that bedevil many children in high-poverty schools like Brighter Choice: unstable housing and chronic health problems that lead to high rates of absences.

Even before Keesha's first PTA meeting that fall, Mr. Daniel was concerned about the 24 children who had missed the first 2 days of school—an early warning sign of chronic absenteeism and poor academic performance. Children who miss a few days in September are likely to miss a full month of the school year, research shows. Even missing a few days each month in kindergarten and 1st grade leads to cascading academic problems. (1)

At a meeting in his office on the third day of school, Mr. Daniel passed around a list of children who were absent to his "attendance team": Bradford Frederick, the attendance teacher; Yolanda Cintron, the social worker; and Ms. Deittra, the parent coordinator.

Ms. Cintron said one child missed school because he was with his mother applying for emergency shelter at the city's PATH intake center in the Bronx (as the office of Prevention and Temporary Housing is known), a process that typically takes a few days; he would miss more days for court hearings as part of a domestic violence case. Three other families, all with parents who were employed, had recently lost their apartments—the details as to exactly what happened weren't clear. But they had been assigned to homeless shelters far away, in the Bronx and Queens, which may account for why their children weren't in school.

The fact that parents who are employed wind up in the shelter system is one more sign of the widening gap between wages and rent in an ever-more-expensive city. Indeed, nearly one third of the families in New York City shelters have a parent who is working. Mostly women, these parents may work as security guards, home health aides, or sales clerks—jobs with wages that are too low to pay New York City's sky-high rents. (2)

Two children who missed the first 2 days of school were in the Dominican Republic on an extended family vacation—a common occurrence among families who try to travel at off-peak times to save money on airfare.

Another child's mother had died, and his father had taken him to Jamaica to visit relatives.

Mr. Frederick said the families of three children had apparently moved out of state over the summer without informing the school; they would be taken off the enrollment rolls as soon as he could confirm their whereabouts.

The numbers were daunting. The previous year, nearly 40% of the children at Brighter Choice were chronically absent; that is, they missed at least a month of the 10-month school year. That number was on a par with other schools in the district but far worse than the citywide average.

Sadly, poor attendance can drag down academic performance not only for the children who miss school, but also for those who attend regularly.

That's because teachers tend to slow the pace of instruction or divert their attention to help children who come to school irregularly. Even the best teachers have trouble ensuring that all children master their lessons when there is a different group of children in the classroom each day. (3)

Chronic absenteeism is a hidden and persistent problem that's often masked by a school's average attendance rate. A school can have average daily attendance of 90% and still have 40% of its students chronically absent, because on different days, different students make up that 90%. (4) That was the case at Brighter Choice.

Some children had health problems like chronic asthma that made them miss school. Asthma disproportionately affects Black and Latino children, who have less access to health care and are more likely to live in housing with conditions, such as cockroaches or mold, that trigger attacks. In Bedford-Stuyvesant, children make *twice* as many emergency room visits for asthma, per capita, as children in Brooklyn on the whole, according to the city health department. (5) Researchers have also found that neighborhoods with high concentrations of public housing have higher rates of asthma and blame mold, poor air quality, and inadequate maintenance. (6) And a child's home is not the only source of asthma triggers: Allergens are also found in some high-poverty schools, although not, thankfully, at Brighter Choice.

At the meeting in Mr. Daniel's office, staff members discussed ways to improve attendance. The attendance teacher and social worker said they would call parents and sometimes make home visits. Someone suggested prizes—maybe a popcorn party for classes in which the children had 100% attendance. Mr. Daniel said he hopes fun activities for children and adults will encourage children to come to school regularly.

"If we open our doors and get families engaged, that will lead to higher attendance," Mr. Daniel told me.

The first week of October, Mr. Daniel invited me to attend another meeting, this time with the School Implementation Team, a group of teachers charged with helping children with significant academic or behavioral problems.

The teachers discussed a handful of children who were having difficulties. One child, his teacher said, kept getting up in the middle of class and leaving the room. Another student, who had significant developmental delays, was falling far behind his classmates. A third had done well in kindergarten, but in 1st grade he began to balk at sitting still and lashed out at his teachers and other children. "He wants to destroy the school and the kids in the class," the teacher said. "He doesn't like the hard seat. He says, 'I don't want to sit all day long.'" That day, Mr. Daniel called the boy's father, who came to the school to pick him up, while the team pondered what to do next. Perhaps he needed neurological testing, and what's called a "one-on-one para," an aide who would sit with him all day. Perhaps he needed to be moved to a special education class.

Of course, all schools must deal with children with behavior problems. But the stress of living in poverty can make children particularly vulnerable. Many poor children face the risk of violence in the home or the community; others live with the constant worry that their parents can't pay the bills. Trauma and chronic stress, a social worker told me, play out in the classroom with an inability to concentrate, undesirable behavior, stomach aches, and headaches.

By early October, the list of children who had excessive lateness or absences had grown to 11 pages. Fifty-six children, nearly one fifth of the school, were either living in shelters or doubled up with friends. Rising rents, a constant issue in a gentrifying neighborhood, were making it increasingly difficult for families to find a place to stay.

Ms. Cintron was trying to get reliable transportation for the children of three families who had been assigned to homeless shelters in the Bronx and Queens. These may seem like curious placements, since there are three homeless shelters within the Brighter Choice attendance zone. However, because vacancies in shelters are scarce, fully half of the city's homeless families are assigned to shelters outside their home borough.

Under law, children have two options for schooling when they become homeless. They may enroll at a new school near their temporary housing, or they may continue to attend their old school, with busing provided by the city. Both options have drawbacks. Changing schools, especially midyear, is disruptive. Shelter placements sometimes last only a few months, so a child who chooses to attend school near the shelter may have to transfer multiple times. Staying in your old school, with friends and familiar teachers and routines, can be a source of comfort and stability for a homeless child. On the other hand, the subway ride from a shelter in the Bronx or Queens to Brighter Choice might take more than 2 hours. And the city's yellow school bus service is famously erratic.

Yellow school buses pick up children from multiple locations and wend their way through the city, dropping them at dozens of different schools, often miles from their homes. Because of the long distances and many stops on school bus routes, children at the far-flung shelters might be picked up as early as 5 A.M. for the long ride to Brighter Choice. Not surprisingly, they often miss the bus.

Without the bus, it was nearly impossible to get to school from the Bronx or Queens. Ms. Cintron, the Brighter Choice staffer charged with helping families in temporary housing, called the Department of Education's Office of Pupil Transportation (OPT) to complain about the early pick-ups but got no response. "That's just the way OPT works," she told the other members of the attendance team at their October meeting.

Children living in shelters may have erratic school attendance not only because of problems with busing, but also because they must accompany their parents to the homeless housing office for multiple appointments to prove their eligibility for assistance. Some must appear in court for domestic violence cases. (During the COVID-19 epidemic of 2020, the city would waive the requirement that homeless children appear in person and permitted verification by video calls instead.)

Shocking as it may seem, the number of homeless families at Brighter Choice is not unusual for high-poverty schools. Some 140 public schools in New York City have homeless rates that top 20%. During the 2018–2019 school year, more than 114,000 children, or one in ten public school pupils, were at some time living in homeless shelters or doubled up with friends or relatives. (7)

How did this happen? Family homelessness has its roots in the changes in both the economy and in public policy in the 1980s. As industrial jobs disappeared, wages stagnated and failed to keep pace with rising rents. The federal government got out of the business of building new subsidized housing and renovating existing properties and began to provide rental vouchers instead. The supply of low-income housing shrank.

The federal budget for housing assistance declined from $19 billion in 1976 to $11 billion in the 1990s. (New York City, to its credit, built and rehabilitated housing on its own. Mayor Ed Koch dedicated $5.1 billion to renovate 250,000 units beginning in 1987.) Single men had once made up the bulk of the homeless population, but by the late 1980s, two thirds of the people staying in shelters were families with children, mostly headed by single mothers. The gap between declining income and rising rents grew still further after the Clinton administration slashed federal welfare benefits for families in 1996. Skyrocketing housing prices during Mayor Mike Bloomberg's administration exacerbated the situation. From 2002 to 2014, the number of homeless families in New York City grew 83%. (8) In the same period, housing costs for poor families were increasing nationwide. By 2013, the majority of poor families in the United States paid more than half their income in rent; one in four paid more than 70%. (9)

At Brighter Choice, it's not only the homeless children who have poor attendance. One child who lived across the street from the school was frequently absent because of asthma. Another child, who had been held back the previous year because of excessive absences, had a mother who didn't seem to understand the seriousness of missing so much school. And it wasn't just the poorest children missing school. Middle-class parents would take their children out of school for family vacations. In schools with high rates of chronic absenteeism, poor attendance can become accepted as ordinary. Parents, children, and school staff all begin to think it's OK to miss some school. (10)

At the same time, demographics aren't destiny. Research shows that school climate matters: that cheerful, welcoming schools have better attendance than gloomy, punitive places. The skill of individual teachers matters, too. Despite high rates of chronic absenteeism overall, several teachers at Brighter Choice had near perfect attendance. One of these was Kim Nunes, the 5th-grade teacher who received a Blackboard Award from *New York Family* magazine in 2019 in recognition of her strength in teaching math.

Ms. Nunes's classroom, with 17 children enrolled, was inviting when I visited in the fall of 2019. The center of the room is devoted to a classroom library, with a plush red carpet surrounded on three sides by shelves stuffed with small plastic bins of fun-to-read books, attractively displayed. Neat bulletin boards displayed children's work. When the children were not sitting on the rug, they sat at tables around the perimeter of the classroom, sometimes working in small groups, sometimes listening as Ms. Nunes explained a lesson.

Ms. Nunes, whose class attendance topped 98% in the fall of 2019 (and whose own children attended Brighter Choice), has strategies to get children excited about school.

She gives her pupils responsibilities she calls "jobs." The "receptionist" answers the landline phone in the classroom on the rare occasions that it rings. The "electrician" makes sure iPads are fully charged and that lights are out at the end of the day. The "librarian" keeps classroom books in order. The "technician" keeps track of classroom laptops. The "distributor" passes out papers. The jobs rotate each month.

She asks their opinions: Where do they want to work? How do they want to work? She makes the classroom feel like a community, family. The children get to use their voice and talk about things. Class is fun.

Each day, she tells them about the lessons planned for the next day—partly to make sure they are prepared, partly to get them excited about coming in. She'll say, "We're working on this project. You'll want to do it." Or she'll remind them they'll be writing songs with the music teacher.

Brighter Choice, like all schools, has teachers with a range of experience and expertise. Ms. Nunes, for example, has been teaching in the city's public schools since she graduated from college in 2002.

Brighter Choice has a word-of-mouth reputation as a collegial place to teach, and teachers seem happy to work there. Teachers responding to annual Department of Education surveys consistently give the school high marks as a place with a supportive environment where staff members trust one another and work collaboratively.

But, like most high-poverty schools, Brighter Choice has fewer experienced teachers than what's typical in schools serving higher-income neighborhoods. Just half of Brighter Choice's teachers had more than 3 years' experience in 2019–2020, compared to 80% citywide. That's significant because children tend to do better in school if they have seasoned teachers. Not all teachers improve with experience, of course. But, on average, the pupils of experienced teachers not only have higher test scores, they also have better attendance, fewer discipline problems, and are more likely to read for pleasure and complete their homework. (11)

High poverty schools tend to have trouble recruiting and retaining teachers. At Brighter Choice, it's hard to replace teachers who leave, despite the school's good reputation.

"It's hard to recruit," a teacher on the hiring committee told me. "When we're looking for teachers, they ask: 'Oh, where's your school located?' So as soon as we say, 'Bedford-Stuyvesant,' they'll say, 'Oh I wanted something closer to home' or, 'Oh, I'm not too sure.' So, there's still like a stigma, you know, in District 16, or just Bed-Stuy schools in general."

At the November 2019 meeting of the School Leadership Team, several parents raised concerns that the school's academics weren't demanding enough, as reflected in the children's poor scores on standardized tests. In 2018, nearly half, or 47%, of the children tested met state standards for reading and math; by 2019 the number had dropped to 38% for math and 33% for reading—well below the citywide rate of 46% for math and 47% for reading. To be sure, test scores are a narrow and limited measure of what children are learning. Particularly at small schools, the results may fluctuate from year to year based on the scores of just a few children. But test scores are one of the few publicly available measures of student progress, and parents at the SLT focused on them.

Delving into the results, the parents found much of the decline could be attributed to the scores among 3rd-graders. A 3rd-grade teacher had left the school several months before children took the state test. Her replacement lasted just 1 week. For the rest of the year, the class had to make do with a series of substitutes—and children apparently didn't learn the skills they needed for the test. A rotating roster of substitutes cannot provide the continuity and consistency children need to make progress.

Teacher turnover isn't the only disruption to the makeup of the classroom. Children also come and go during the school year. As a zoned public school, Brighter Choice admits any child who arrives midyear—15 in the first semester of 2019, half of whom were living in shelters. That means the children who are tested in the spring aren't necessarily the same as the children who started school in September. A further difficulty: The school's budget is based on the number of children who are enrolled as of October 31 each year. The school receives no money for children who enroll after that date. The administration must stretch the school's existing budget to accommodate the midyear arrivals, who often have more learning difficulties than children with stable housing.

Mr. Daniel told parents at the SLT meeting about his strategy for boosting test scores. The school would start Saturday test prep sessions as early as December 7 for children who needed extra help—more than one month earlier than the previous year. He invited parents to volunteer on Saturday to work with children one-on-one who might be having trouble reading. Someone suggested a pep rally to boost the spirits of children before the testing days. Mr. Daniel was upbeat as usual, showing no sign that he was discouraged by the herculean efforts needed to boost attendance and strengthen the school's academic program.

The calendar year 2020 got off to a promising start. Mr. Daniel seemed to have won over the staff and the parents. Mr. Daniel was correct that the fun activities of the fall would engage families and build a sense of community. Mr. Daniel was popular with teachers, who felt he always had their back, and he had a winning way with the children. He tried to be responsive to everyone. He was always accessible, responding quickly when parents texted him on his cellphone.

For once, there were no complaints voiced at the January meetings of the School Leadership Team or the PTA—unlike the fall semester, when parents challenged everything from the rigor of the curriculum to Mr. Daniel's decision to send children outdoors for recess on a particularly cold day. Instead, there were productive conversations about plans for Black History Month in February and praise for improvements in Spanish instruction in the dual-language classes. Teachers began offering Saturday morning classes for children who needed extra help, and some parents seemed optimistic that this enrichment would boost the school's lagging test scores. Saturday morning "skate club" continued to be a popular time for parents and children to gather on the playground. The school year seemed to be shaping up well.

The PTA candy sale raised enough money to send the entire 5th-grade class on a two-night trip in January to Frost Valley, the YMCA environmental center 3½ hours' drive north of the city. The children and their teachers stayed in cabins, hiked in the snow, and learned about the environment. Twenty-nine of the school's 36 5th-graders went; the remaining children's parents were hesitant to send their children so far from home. There had been some complaints from parents who objected to selling candy—rather than a healthier alternative—and Talia was worn out from keeping track of which children had paid for the hundreds of boxes of candy that had been distributed, but all in all it was a successful event.

On the morning of February 28, parents gathered in the auditorium for the celebration of Black History Month, a culmination of schoolwide social studies projects. Before parents walked the halls to see student work, several stood to give shout-outs to the teachers and staff who organized the event, and the auditorium burst into applause.

Mr. Daniel rose to speak. "We can all benefit by learning history that has been hidden or whitewashed for years," he said. "There will be some things you might see that you disagree with. Not everything's going to be perfect. And I'm a little bit scared." In a school where sensitivities can be raw, there was reason for him to be nervous. But in this case his anxiety was misplaced.

As parents fanned out to see the children's classrooms, the children stood proudly in front of their poster-board projects, explaining what they had learned. One class had studied the African American artist Jacob Lawrence, who chronicled the Great Migration of Black Americans to the North. Children created their own artwork inspired by his paintings. Another class had assembled posters telling the story of Ruby Bridges, the first Black child to desegregate an all-White school in New Orleans, in 1960. As parents stood by, the children recounted what they had learned. "We are brave like Ruby," one child said. "People threw garbage at her," said another.

Still another class re-enacted the legal battles to desegregate schools, with one child dressed as a judge, other children carrying cardboard signs saying, "No coloreds allowed," and still others dressed as U.S. marshals escorting a Black child to school. "History was made for all mankind when Blacks and Whites could go to school together," one child said.

History wasn't sugar-coated. Ms. Nunes's 5th-grade class compared living conditions in the South and the North during the Great Migration. The students learned that while Black individuals who moved North were able to vote and found better paying jobs, they also faced severe discrimination.

It was also clear the staff was trying to include Spanish speakers in the Black History celebration. In one class, children performed a skit about José Celso Barbosa, the first Puerto Rican and one the first people of African descent to earn a medical degree in the United States. In another class, children danced to a song by Celia Cruz, the Cuban American Queen of Salsa. The contributions of White Americans to the Civil Rights movement were noted as well: Fifth-graders pointed out that Black and White Freedom Riders faced violence and jail in 1961 in their quest to desegregate buses.

At the first PTA meeting in September, Keesha had promised parents the school would continue to promote African American culture while learning to include other cultures as well. The Gallery Walk, as the event was called, seemed to fulfill that promise. The atmosphere was buoyant as parents lingered in the halls, eating snacks and chatting with one another. Parents left the school by mid-morning, proud of their children's accomplishments.

But tensions were simmering within the PTA. Keesha was increasingly irritated by what she saw as Talia's abrasive, take-charge attitude. And Talia was increasingly irritated by what she saw as Keesha's habitual lateness and her inability to take responsibility for PTA projects. The friction came to a head after the Black History Month celebration, in the evening at Family Movie Night on February 28.

Talia and Lauren had been in the habit of arriving early to help set up tables, make popcorn, get the cashbox out, and sell tickets. But Talia, worn out by her other responsibilities as PTA treasurer, had asked Keesha if she could find someone else to take care of the set-up for movie night. Keesha had agreed.

So, Talia was irritated when she arrived at the school at 5:30 P.M., an hour in advance of the 6:30 P.M. screening of *Mad Hot Ballroom,* and Keesha was nowhere to be seen. Other parents turned to Talia to ask what needed to be done to set up the auditorium and the lobby outside. Talia felt Keesha had let her down and dumped an unwanted responsibility on her.

When Keesha arrived 40 minutes later, Talia raised her voice, in front of other parents and children: "You deal with this! I really said I didn't want to do it."

There were some cold stares, but no one wanted to spoil the movie for the children, so the grown-ups went grumpily but quietly to their seats.

Afterwards, Keesha assembled the board of the PTA, including Talia, in the lobby. "Listen, you know, sometimes things are going to upset us," she said. "But if there's a problem, and you need to discuss it with me, the only thing I'm going to ask is that you allow me to get into the school building, before you ambush me. I don't believe our business should be held at the entrance of the school. We can go to the office and then we'll talk. We'll hash it out. We will figure out what the resolution is." She thanked Lauren and Talia for their work, and said their help was no longer needed.

Talia was infuriated. "I have a temper, and I'm sure there was a better way to handle it," she told me later. "But I had asked for help, and then, instead of getting the help, I got publicly reprimanded like a toddler in front of people and told off. I was told my help wasn't needed and I was like, 'Oh, if you don't need my help, I'll just leave.'"

She texted her resignation as treasurer before Movie Night was over.

In the next few days, Frances, the PTA vice president, tried to mediate the dispute between Keesha and Talia. But, as Frances told me later, she was dealing with two strong-willed women, and nothing came of her efforts.

The falling out between Keesha and Talia was a clear case of expecting too much from people whose lives were already too busy. All working parents—mothers especially—are tired by the time Friday night rolls around, and Keesha and Talia were both exhausted. Both had spent many hours of unpaid time working for the PTA, and both had demanding full-time jobs and small children to care for. Perhaps it was unrealistic to expect the PTA to raise money for the 5th-grade class trip to Frost Valley—a task that wore Talia out. Perhaps it was unrealistic to expect a PTA president with a full-time job to attend numerous meetings of the PTA, the SLT, the Title 1 committee, and a district-wide group called the Presidents Council, as Keesha had done.

It surely had been unrealistic for the PTA to rely on volunteer labor to organize an after-school program for 3- and 4-year-olds—as it had tried to do the year before. That onerous task had tempted the previous PTA president to try to turn the after-school program into a private business—a move that had caused so much friction when money disappeared from the PTA bank account. Luckily, the school administration hired an outside contractor to run the after-school for the youngest children in the fall of 2019, so the PTA was no longer responsible. But Talia was still bitter about the experience of the previous year.

Even with a committed group of parents, Brighter Choice's PTA is no match for the high-powered, high-budget PTAs in wealthier neighborhoods, where parents raise money not just for nice extras but also for the salaries of teaching assistants and for programs such as music, art, and sports. However well-meaning these efforts are, they widen the gaps between the haves and the have-nots. As sociologist Linn Posey-Maddox has observed, relying on parent volunteers unfairly shifts the responsibility for high-quality schooling from government to individuals. (12) Keesha and Talia had run into a problem that has bedeviled public education in New York City for years: Good schools cannot be built fairly on the unpaid labor of overworked mothers. In their mostly successful efforts to build a warm community at Brighter Choice, Keesha and Talia had pushed themselves to exhaustion.

One day after the Movie Night quarrel, at 2:00 A.M. on a Sunday morning, March 1, Keesha heard a strange noise. Something sounded like rain. She heard a pitter-patter, crackling sound on the ceiling of their apartment, the second floor of a three-family house.

She woke Keyonn.

"He's like, 'You hear that?' I was like, 'Yeah, I don't know what that is,'" she told me later. Keyonn went upstairs to investigate. Smoke billowed from the upstairs apartment. Keesha called the fire department, then Keesha, Keyonn, and Little Keyonn got out just as the ceiling of their apartment crashed in. The noise they had heard, the noise that sounded like rain, was a fire headed their way from the apartment upstairs.

It was 7:00 A.M. by the time the fire was fully extinguished, and Keesha and her family had given their statements to the police and fire departments. An electrical short might have caused the fire, but police also told them they had responded to a case of domestic violence at the upstairs apartment the afternoon before and speculated the two events might be related.

Whatever the cause, property fires are yet another danger that disproportionately affect African Americans, who are twice as likely to die in fires as members of other racial groups. Black Americans are more likely to live in poorly maintained housing with conditions that may lead to fires, such as faulty electrical systems or inadequate heating that leads tenants to use space heaters. Two thirds of the rental housing in Bedford-Stuyvesant has at least one maintenance defect, according to the Department of Health. (13)

When the fire was out, the firefighters let the family collect a few belongings. Little Keyonn's school uniforms and some winter clothes were all they could salvage from the ruined apartment. A representative from the Red Cross was on hand to offer emergency housing but advised the family to wait until nighttime because it could only pay for two nights in a hotel. Arriving at the hotel before the afternoon check-in time would mean they could only stay for one night.

So, instead of going straight to the hotel, Keesha, Keyonn, and Little Keyonn went to Keesha's sister's apartment in the public housing development where Keesha had grown up, in the adjacent neighborhood of East New York. It was nice to be around family, and Little Keyonn was able to play with his two cousins. But the two-bedroom apartment was too small for all of them to stay for long. That evening they drove to the hotel assigned to them by the Red Cross. Next door was a men's shelter. On the street outside, homeless guys wandered, prostitutes solicited customers, and dealers sold drugs. They so feared leaving their car on the street that they drove back to Keesha's sister's house, parked the car there, and took an Uber to the hotel.

"You know, we don't have a Mercedes-Benz or anything," Keesha told me. "We have a little beat-up car. So, if I didn't want to leave a little beat-up poopy car in this area that gives you an idea of the area that we're in. I was like. 'No, sir. No, no, no.'"

Once inside, the hotel room was safe and clean enough, with a bathroom and a microwave and a little stove. On Monday morning, Little Keyonn was back at school.

But memories of the fire would haunt her. "The effects last longer than you'll ever imagine," she told me months later. Whenever it rained, she would get anxious. It took her a little while to realize why: The sound of rain reminded her of the sound of the fire coming through the ceiling of her apartment.

The fire had a lasting effect on Little Keyonn, too.

"We tried to keep things as normal as possible for Little Keyonn and it seemed like he was moving through it with no problems or no issues," Keesha said. "But Big Keyonn said he overheard him having a conversation with his grandmother about nightmares. And the nightmares have to do with fires. We thought we kept it good for him. But even in all of that he was still affected."

In the days right after the fire, they scrambled to find a place to stay—first another hotel in Downtown Brooklyn, then a friend's apartment that was used as an Airbnb. But their own troubles were soon overshadowed by global events that would reverberate in New York City and test the community Keesha had helped to build at Brighter Choice.

EIGHT

COVID-19 Tests the Community

Kristina Bumphrey/ Kristina B. Photography

A Black Lives Matter demonstration brought the community together after a terrifying spring.

If Keesha's life was hard when her apartment was destroyed, it would get even harder in the next weeks and months. On March 1, 2020, the same day as the fire, New York State had its first confirmed case of COVID-19. By mid-April of 2020, New York had become the epicenter of the global pandemic, and the state was averaging more than 900 deaths a day. (1)

Keesha, Keyonn, and Little Keyonn hunkered down in their friends' apartment. They ventured outside only once a week to buy groceries and cleaning supplies that weren't available for online delivery. The constant sirens from ambulances ferrying patients to Interfaith Medical Center, two blocks away from their friend's apartment, terrified them. So did the sight of tents set up outside the hospital to care for patients for whom there were no beds inside.

"I felt like we were in a war zone," Keesha told me afterward. "Ambulances were always going. You saw them every day. You heard them every night. It was probably one of the most scariest feelings I've ever had."

All three members of the family had asthma—which put them at higher risk of COVID-19. In addition, Keesha suffered from heart trouble, and her surgery had to be postponed because of the pandemic.

Things that had seemed so pressing a few months earlier—raising money for the Frost Valley trip, organizing Family Movie Night, finding ways to boost test scores—seemed trivial compared to the challenge of simply staying alive.

After the bad luck of having their apartment burn down, Keesha and Keyonn had the good luck of a stable place to stay. They had originally planned on staying just a few days in the friends' apartment, which was usually rented on Airbnb. As the pandemic intensified and the prospect of short-term bookings dimmed, their friends agreed to give them a one-year lease. Other friends had tried to organize a party at a local restaurant to raise money to replace the belongings lost in the fire, but the party was canceled because of the pandemic. Instead, their friends organized a GoFundMe campaign that raised more than $10,000.

As the pandemic wore on, Big Keyonn and Keesha were both able to work remotely, saving them from the risk of going out—and the loss of income from being laid off. It was tough sharing space in the two-bedroom apartment, but their two-family house had a backyard. The owners, who lived upstairs, had two children who had gone to nursery school with Little

Keyonn. The children played together and enjoyed the trampoline in the backyard.

There were losses and disappointments big and small. Little Keyonn, an outgoing child with a theatrical bent, had just been cast as Aladdin in the school's musical theater production. He was sad that the show was canceled. He missed his daily hug from the school safety agent, J. Brown, who used to greet children as they entered the school. He missed his mother's PTA meetings—because that was a time he could play with friends at school and eat pizza without too much structure or supervision. Still, Keesha's family was safe for now and no one contracted the virus.

Other Brighter Choice families were not so lucky.

Nadia Licona, a kindergartner at Brighter Choice, contracted COVID-19 in March 2020. At first, the little girl, whose mother works in a restaurant and whose father works in construction, had a fever. Then she complained of a pain in her stomach. Then she had trouble breathing.

"She said, 'Mommy, take me to the hospital,'" her mother, Susana Sanchez, an immigrant from Mexico, told me later. They took a taxi to Woodhull Hospital Center, a city hospital in Bedford-Stuyvesant. An X-ray revealed a severe case of pneumonia. One lung was three quarters filled with fluid, the other was completely full.

The little girl was transferred to Bellevue Hospital in Manhattan, where she was put in a coma and placed on a ventilator so doctors could extract fluid from her lungs. After 12 days in a coma and 20 days in the hospital, she returned home. Although she recovered, she would be dogged by fears for months.

"Before, she never cried. She was brave," her mother told me when we met on the playground at Brighter Choice more than a year later. "Now she is sensitive. She always cries."

Ms. Brown, the school safety agent, who has asthma, also contracted COVID-19. As members of the police department, school safety agents were required to report to work throughout the pandemic, even when the schools were closed. In the beginning of the ordeal, before face masks were recommended and widely available, they were often exposed to the virus. Ms. Brown went to Brookdale Hospital when she first had symptoms, but she was turned away because the hospital was overwhelmed with even sicker patients. Later, when her temperature spiked and she had trouble breathing, her grown son called an ambulance. This time, she was admitted to Kings County Hospital, where she stayed for a month, one night on a ventilator.

"There were people screaming for help in the hospital, and every minute you'd hear 'code blue, code blue,'" she told me later, using the hospital term for a medical emergency such as a cardiac arrest. Her supervisor in the police department died. And, although Ms. Brown recovered, she would suffer ill effects for many months. A year later, she told me she was still short of breath and was seeing a counselor to cope with the trauma. When she watched the news on television, she would have flashbacks to her time in the hospital.

The pandemic hit some communities much harder than others. Black and Latino Americans were dying at much higher rates than White Americans, for a number of reasons: They were more likely to have health conditions like asthma that made them more vulnerable; they were more likely to live in cramped quarters where the virus spread fastest; and they were more likely to have jobs that required them to work in person—jobs as home-health aides, or grocery clerks, or transit workers, or delivery men—jobs that had been undervalued before the pandemic and that now were considered "essential." COVID-19 exposed longstanding health disparities between racial groups and a health care system that favored the wealthy. Hospitals in poor and working-class neighborhoods were quickly overwhelmed. Some health care workers couldn't even get personal protective equipment such as masks and gowns. "In the Upper East Side of Manhattan hospitals, you could get full access to anything, but in Queens and Brooklyn we had people wearing garbage bags because they couldn't get surgical gowns," a union official for hospital workers told the *Financial Times*. (2)

There wasn't much help from Washington. President Donald Trump dismissed the threat of COVID-19, suggesting it was no worse than the flu and in any case would miraculously disappear. The Centers for Disease Control initially created flawed COVID tests—and forbade private labs from conducting their own tests. It issued confusing advice on masks, at first suggesting masks were unnecessary for the general public.

Without federal guidance or support, cities and states were on their own to figure out what to do. Turf battles and bickering between Gov. Andrew Cuomo and Mayor Bill de Blasio added to the confusion. Parents and teachers were left to struggle with confusing and contradictory dictates from Albany and City Hall.

The mayor initially resisted closing the city's public schools, even as COVID-19 cases mounted, and private schools and universities closed. Ignoring the pleas of his own Health Department, he cited the importance of schools to low-income families for childcare and meals. It was only on March 15, when the Health Department gave de Blasio forecasts suggesting tens of thousands of people might die if restrictions were not imposed, that de Blasio relented and ordered the schools closed. (3)

Faced with a terrifying pandemic and little help from the city or state, Brighter Choice staff, teachers, and parent volunteers mobilized to feed the children in their care, to make sure they were safe, and to supply them with books and computers. As they confronted heartbreaking situations, members of the community pulled together to help one another. But the disruptions to schooling were profound and not easily overcome.

In the days after de Blasio canceled in-person classes, the teachers came to school and scoured the building for extra laptops and iPads so that children could continue their lessons online. Staff members and parent volunteers set up folding tables outside for parents to pick up worksheets and homework packets, along with the laptops and iPads.

Mr. Daniel texted just about every family to make sure they were okay. He held frequent "town hall" meetings—online video chats with parents. Some teachers went to homeless shelters in person to drop off homework packets. The school cafeteria never closed. Cafeteria workers came to school throughout the pandemic, preparing sandwiches and snacks that anyone in the neighborhood could take away for free. More than ever, Brighter Choice was not just a place to teach children to read and write. It was the source of strength and the center of the community.

The best teachers at Brighter Choice came up with creative ways to teach online even as they struggled to care for their own children at home. One teacher offered flamenco dance classes. Another led the children in African drumming and dance. The science teacher held an online workshop for parents to help children design projects for a virtual science fair. The gym teacher offered virtual workout classes with his own children from his living room on GoogleMeet, an online platform similar to Zoom. Ms. Deittra, the parent coordinator, organized "restorative circles," morale-boosting meetings where the children could see their classmates on the video call and talk about how they were feeling, what they missed, and what they longed for.

But some teachers didn't offer live instruction—they just posted worksheets online and never interacted with the children at all. And at least one teacher gave up trying. One father told me his son's teacher couldn't figure out how to "mute" the class during a video call. When the children unmuted themselves and started talking to one another, ignoring the teacher, the teacher simply walked away. One of the children took over and led the lesson.

Some parents fell back on their own resources, improvising homeschooling to fill the gaps. Talia and her son Rian, who lived on the bottom two floors of the four-story house she owns, teamed up with Lauren and her daughter, Luna, who rented the fourth-floor apartment. They made a school room in Talia's apartment; the two mothers took turns watching the children, squeezing their own work in as best they could. Talia's sister offered art classes via Zoom. Her mother in Toronto read aloud to the children on a video chat. Lauren's sister offered a drama class. They hired a tutor in Peru to give live instruction in Spanish via the Internet.

Not all parents had the resources to homeschool their children, and, with the schools closed, the pandemic would widen the gap between children with ample help to learn at home and the neediest children who lacked both WiFi connections and parents who could help with lessons. Some of the most vulnerable children simply disappeared. Ms. Cintron, the social worker, tried to maintain contact with the school's homeless children; she lost touch with a few. Their parents' cellphones were disconnected, and teachers had no way of finding them. School had been a source of stability for children in temporary housing. Now, even that fragile stability was gone.

On May 25, 2020, the nation was horrified by the police killing of an unarmed Black man, George Floyd, in Minneapolis. The killing, captured on video by a bystander, unleashed a torrent of rage across the country and sparked the largest demonstrations in U.S. history, with 15 million to 26 million people taking to the streets proclaiming, "Black lives matter!" (4)

In New York City, the marches went on for days, across all five boroughs. The protestors were largely peaceful, but some clashed with police, set fire to police cars, hurled bottles, and smashed windows. For their part, some police officers charged and swung batons at peaceful demonstrators, seemingly with little provocation. (5)

At Brighter Choice, children and parents gathered for their own Black Lives Matter march. It was the first time the community had come together in person since the COVID-19 pandemic began. Mr. Daniel, a yellow bandana covering his nose and mouth, and a bullhorn in hand, led several dozen children, parents, and teachers on a short march from the school entrance around the corner to the school's playground, where the children held up homemade cardboard signs reading "Black Lives Matter!" and "Las Vidas Negras Importante!" Everyone was carefully masked, with each family standing a safe 6 feet from the next. Mr. Daniel held up a cellphone and livestreamed the event for 40 other people who joined online. "Social distance, please!" he shouted. On the playground, children and adults, Black, White, and Hispanic, chanted: "Black lives matter! Racism has no place here!

"No justice, no peace! The people united will never be defeated!"

It was a cathartic moment, a chance to bring the community together with a pledge to fight racism after a terrifying spring. Whatever other problems they might have, the parents, teachers, and children felt they had one another. Even with the classrooms closed, Brighter Choice was teaching children important lessons, such as how to be kind to one another. The school was building a community of mutual respect among both adults and children.

The march fell on June 19, or Juneteenth, the anniversary of the day in 1865 when the U.S. Army landed in Galveston, Texas, with the news that the Civil War was over and enslaved people there were free. Juneteenth, long celebrated in the African American community, had never been recognized as a national holiday. On its own, the community at Brighter Choice had decided to commemorate it.

By the end of June, the first peak of the pandemic had passed. The summer promised to be less frightening than the spring had been. A few of the city's public swimming pools were open, and the pool in Bedford-Stuyvesant offered some respite for families with young children. Keesha began venturing out of her apartment more often, taking Little Keyonn to play in the local parks.

Some weeks before, she had taken a leave of absence from her job. Her heart surgery had been postponed indefinitely because of the pandemic, and she needed to do whatever she could to reduce stress that exacerbated her condition. With schools closed, someone needed to take care of Little

Keyonn during the day. Even without a full-time job, she had enough on her plate.

But just as the fear of COVID-19 was receding, another threat loomed. Crime was rising, and some worried the city would return to the bad old days of the 1980s when gang fights to control the crack trade took hundreds of lives. Citywide, the number of shootings nearly doubled compared to the year before. Eight people were killed in a single day. (6)

A particularly chilling case horrified and saddened the Bedford-Stuyvesant community. Just before midnight July 12, in a playground half a mile from Brighter Choice, two men jumped out of an SUV and began shooting indiscriminately into a crowd at a family cookout. Three men were injured in what police said was a fight between rival gangs.

A stray bullet shot and killed a 22-month-old boy, Davell Gardner, sitting in his stroller. (7) His family lived in a homeless shelter near Brighter Choice. His older sister was a pupil at the school.

For Keesha, the killing, just three blocks from her old apartment, was a worrisome sign that police were pulling back in the wake of the Black Lives Matter protests. In earlier months, she had frequently walked by the site of the shooting on her way to pick up pizza from a neighborhood restaurant. The playground was an apparent trouble spot for gang activity, and there had always been a police car parked there as a deterrent. But since the Black Lives Matter demonstrations had begun, the police had disappeared.

"That's just painful," she told me on a Zoom call. "That's the response to people being killed unjustly? It results in you not wanting to do your job?"

It's impossible to tie the shooting directly to the presence or absence of police patrols, of course. Crime typically goes up in the summer and, long before the COVID-19 pandemic or the Black Lives Matter demonstrations, gang violence was a problem in the neighborhood. Still, as crime spiked, the number of arrests plummeted by more than 60% in New York City, leading some to complain that police were staging a work slowdown. *The New York Times* suggested a "hostile political climate" had made "officers reluctant to carry out arrests because of what they see as unfair scrutiny of their conduct." Budget cuts to the police budget and a move to outlaw chokeholds contributed to low police morale. (8)

"No one is doing anything," a police supervisor in Brooklyn told the *New York Daily News*. "If there's probable cause, we'll make an arrest. And we'll respond to any 911 call. But as far as going the extra yard, that's not happening. Guys are not getting out of their cars. They're not going up to guys on corners." (9)

Community activists and scholars have long noted that neighborhoods like Bedford-Stuyvesant suffer simultaneously from over-policing and under-policing, overly aggressive police tactics and neglect. Like poor health and homelessness, crime and poor policing are conditions outside a school's control. Nonetheless, just as a school must deal with the chronic absenteeism that grows out of poor health and inadequate housing, it must wrestle with the impact that both crime and overly aggressive policing can have on its pupils.

Violence creates anxiety and stress that can affect a whole community—not only the direct victims of crime, but also people living nearby. It can even have an impact on how well children do in school. Researchers at New York University compared reading scores of children who were exposed to a violent crime on their block in the week before a test to those who had not been near a crime: Children who lived near the violent crime scored lower. Stress apparently affects children's ability to concentrate. (10)

At the same time, overly aggressive policing has also been linked to lower achievement. One recent study found Mayor's Bloomberg's policy of "stop-and-frisk" led to higher high school dropout rates among teenagers in precincts where the tactics were the most pronounced. (11) Another study linked aggressive police tactics to lower test scores among Black teenage males in New York City. The mechanisms that lead to the declines are not well understood, but researchers suggest stress plays a role. In addition, unpleasant interactions with police may lead students to mistrust institutions, including schools (whose security officers are part of the police department), leading to chronic absenteeism. (12)

How can Black and Hispanic parents get the police protection they need to keep their children safe, without the hostile interactions with police that have proven all too common? It's a dilemma parents at Brighter Choice had confronted several months earlier, just before the pandemic closed the schools.

At a meeting of the School Leadership Team, an African American mother, concerned about reports of sexual predators in the neighborhood, suggested asking the local police precinct to give children advice on how to protect themselves. But other parents, also African American, had bad experiences with police and didn't trust them to speak to their children. As a compromise, the group agreed to invite a police representative to speak to parents at the next PTA meeting—but not to speak to children directly.

Sgt. James Harper, an African American officer, dressed in plainclothes, came to the January 2020 meeting of the PTA. He told parents of a new police initiative to send "youth community officers" to schools to build trust with young people. The parents were polite but wary.

"Officers don't say 'good morning,' they just stand there," one father said.

"Is there training for officers who don't live in the neighborhood but who work here?" another father asked.

"Is there unconscious bias training?" a mother asked.

Sgt. Harper said officers were being trained in "10 ways to handle a situation." He said there were concerted efforts to change police culture. "It won't happen overnight, but it's happening," he said.

One father suggested an "icebreaker" such as a basketball game between parents and police officers, or "a meet and greet" outside the school. Harper gave parents his phone number and email address.

"We appreciate your time," a mother said. The meeting adjourned.

It's not clear what might have happened had the pandemic not closed the schools, but the meeting with Sgt. Harper and the PTA may have been a baby step toward better relations between the community and the police. As it was, Keesha, for one, felt anger at both police brutality and what she saw as police shirking their duty to protect the neighborhood.

When I spoke to Keesha in August 2020, she told me that the rise in crime over the summer was reminiscent of her own childhood, growing up in the projects in the 1980s during the crack epidemic. One day, when she was out with Little Keyonn and his cousin, there was a drive-by shooting just a few blocks from the park where they were playing.

"It's a perfect storm for this kind of thing," she told me. "This pandemic thing, racial tensions flaring, people were stuck in their homes for weeks. A lot of people lost their jobs. People in houses where, you know, there was already existing domestic issues. So, it is beyond unfortunate, but it's just crazy."

Over the summer of 2020, there was lots of confusion about when school would open in the fall and what safety measures would be put in place.

Although New York City would be one of the few big-city school districts to open its schools, its on-again off-again schedules were so disruptive that it wasn't clear how much learning was taking place.

The city offered parents the choice of "remote learning"—essentially continuing the online lessons the children had during the spring—or "blended learning," where children would be in person at school 2½ days a week, with online lessons the rest of the week. The schedule was designed to decrease the number of children in each class by half and allow enough space to reduce the spread of the virus.

The mayor met a wave of opposition from teachers, who threatened to strike over what they considered inadequate safety measures, and principals, who said they needed time and resources to solve the enormous logistical challenges of scheduling teachers for "blended" or "remote" learning. Twice, the mayor postponed the first day of school. Schools finally began offering "remote" learning on Sept 21. Prekindergartners were allowed to attend in person that day; older children had to wait until Sept. 29.

Through it all, Mr. Daniel was always accessible. He had frequent "town hall" meetings—online video chats with parents—answering their questions when he could and, when he could not, promising to share whatever information he had as soon as he had it. His collegial, can-do attitude bore fruit. When the 2020–2021 school year began, 26 staffers returned to school in person. Just four requested and received medical exemptions to work remotely—well below the citywide rate. Indeed, at a time when many teachers were wary of returning to class, teachers at Brighter Choice agreed to teach their students both ways: online and in person. According to an agreement with the teachers' union, staffers who offered classes in person could not also be required to offer online instruction. But Brighter Choice teachers were willing to be flexible. The staff was willing to go an extra mile for the kids and persevere under difficult circumstances.

Despite everyone's best efforts, though, for many children it was a lost year. Brighter Choice was like a ghost town. Even though nearly all the staff members came to work each day, some classes in the upper grades had only one or two children attending in person. Only 100 children had signed up for "blended learning," and, because most were coming in just 2½ days a week, only about half of those attended in person on any given day. Attendance was an issue both for the children attending school in person and those learning remotely. One teacher told me many children didn't do their homework, or even log on to their computers. It wasn't clear where they were.

During Mr. Daniel's "town hall" video calls, parents complained that online lessons were impossible for children who were too young to type on a keyboard. In any case, the lessons were mostly worksheets and multiple-choice questions about short reading passages.

Some students did have good experiences. Keesha set up a remote-learning "pod" with her upstairs neighbor and two other families whose children, like Keyonn, were in the 3rd grade. The children met at Keesha's house and set up their laptops and iPads for remote lessons from their teachers, who were broadcasting from their classrooms in Brighter Choice. The parents took turns watching the children, who could eat lunch together, do their homework, and play in the backyard after lessons were done. It was a way to get some of the social benefits of school, without the health risks.

Frances, the PTA vice president, and Ibrahim, active in Fathers on a Mission, opted for "blended learning" for their daughter Aissa, in the 2nd grade. By November, she was able to attend class in person 5 days a week, because so few other children were attending school in person. Frances said Aissa benefited from the tiny class size—there were just 10 children in the class—and the family hired a private tutor to help fill in gaps.

Other parents withdrew their children from Brighter Choice. Lurie, the civil rights lawyer who had first raised concerns about gentrification and White supremacy and who had led the School Leadership Team, moved to New Jersey, telling other parents that crime in Bedford-Stuyvesant had become too frightening.

Another African American family enrolled their daughter in Poly Prep Country Day School, a private school in Park Slope. The White father who had lobbied for outdoor recess hired a tutor to homeschool his daughter.

Ms. Nunes, the 5th-grade teacher who had won an award for excellence in math instruction, kept working at the school, but her own children were no longer at Brighter Choice. Her older daughter graduated and began 6th grade at a progressive private school in Bedford-Stuyvesant; her younger daughter, due to start 2nd grade, enrolled there as well.

Two of the most active parents in the PTA, Talia and Lauren, enrolled their children at PS 9, a popular multiracial school in nearby District 13. As PS 9's enrollment had declined when middle-class families left for the suburbs or private schools, there was now room for out-of-district families like Talia's and Lauren's.

Talia had never gotten over the bad feelings around the missing PTA funds the year before, and she felt she and Lauren weren't appreciated on the PTA. When her son's teacher had gone on maternity leave in early 2020, the class had a string of substitutes. The online lessons were disappointing, and her son wasn't learning much.

For Lauren, who had stayed on as PTA secretary after Talia quit as treasurer, the last straw came after a disappointing summer "welcome" video chat with the teacher her daughter, Luna, was to be assigned to in the fall. The teacher said the class would focus on remediation in the coming year because so many children had fallen behind during the pandemic.

"The teacher said, 'I expect all the kids will come in reading below grade level," Lauren said. "It's hard to listen to a teacher say, 'I don't actually expect you to do well.'"

Despite leaving Brighter Choice, Talia and Lauren were still committed to sending their children to a racially integrated school: PS 9 was about one-third White, 40% Black and the rest Latino and Asian. PS 9, with more middle-class children than Brighter Choice, had a well-established PTA and they felt they could be active without becoming exhausted.

The fall of 2020 was a frightening and disorienting time. After a brief period of calm, COVID-19 cases accelerated when the second COVID wave hit. In early September, there were fewer than 300 reported cases a day in New York City. By the first week of November, there were 1,000 cases a day. By the end of November, there were 2,000 a day. By mid-January 2021, there were 6,000 a day. (13)

On Nov. 18, just 8 weeks after children returned to school, the mayor ordered the schools shut. The rate of positive COVID tests in the city had risen to 3%—an arbitrary threshold the mayor and the teachers' union had agreed would trigger school closing citywide. And so, even though restaurants and gyms were still open, and even though schools elsewhere in the state remained open, New York City schools pivoted to online classes for all children. With barely 12 hours' notice, parents once again scrambled to find child care and accommodate remote learning. Ten days later, the mayor announced elementary schools would re-open Dec. 7; middle and high schools were closed indefinitely.

The second COVID-19 wave touched Brighter Choice in tragic ways. The school lost its first staff member to COVID-19 in November: Kelly Allen, a 51-year-old cafeteria worker. Like all cafeteria staff, she had worked in person throughout the pandemic, making take-out breakfasts and lunches for anyone in the community who wanted them. She had arthritis and asthma, making her especially vulnerable to the virus. Despite the risk, she felt obliged to continue working, a colleague told me, because her husband and grown children were out of work and she was the only member of her household with a job.

Three teachers contracted COVID-19 and recovered. But Rebecca Morales, who taught art to children with autism in the school for disabled children that shared a building with Brighter Choice, struggled in the hospital for months. She had asthma, had been teaching remotely, and was careful to limit her exposure, a colleague told me. Nonetheless she contracted COVID-19.

In the spring of 2021, after the second wave had faded and vaccines had become available, Ms. Morales died. "She was the life of the party, the reason everyone got together," her supervisor, Roderick Palton, told me. A single mother, she left a 4-year-old daughter, a prekindergartner at Brighter Choice.

Parents at Brighter Choice heard news of the death at a lunch the PTA organized for Teacher Appreciation Day, one of the first times parents had been in the school building since the pandemic began. Jess, a professional caterer and a member of the PTA executive board, brought trays of pulled pork and laid them out on tables in the school library. Other parents brought baked beans, quinoa, salad, cookies, and brownies. Teachers gathered around, taking their masks off long enough to eat. The food was great, but the atmosphere was subdued. As one mother said as she helped clean up after lunch, "It's hard to keep moving forward surrounded by so much death."

NINE

"Trust Is the Glue"

Clara Hemphill

Fall 2021 brought mostly good news, if not a return to normalcy.

The first day of school is always exciting, but it was particularly exciting in September 2021, when children returned to full-time classes for the first time since the pandemic closed schools in the spring of 2020. Parents, most wearing face masks, exchanged greetings outside the school. Keesha and Brandi, another mother on the PTA board, sold Brighter Choice polo shirts from a table on the sidewalk. Each class lined up to wait for their teachers to take them inside. Even though they wore face masks, it was easy to see that the children were both anxious and happy to reunite with their friends.

The teachers had planned special activities on the playground after lunch to welcome everyone back—a dance-a-thon, field games, a video game truck. But the activities were canceled when the administration received word of gunshots fired just a block from the school. No one was hurt—and the administration never learned exactly what happened—but the police advised everyone to shelter-in-place until the threat subsided.

"It was a wonderful morning and early afternoon, until we had to 'shelter in' due to police activity around the neighborhood!" Mr. Daniel emailed me with his characteristic cup-is-half-full good cheer. School opening was an obstacle course, but, he said, "I'm proud of our response team!"

For Keesha and her son's classmates, it was another disappointment after months of losses big and small. "The school planned some really fun activities, and the shooting took that away from them," she emailed me.

Even so, the fall brought mostly good news, if not a return to normalcy. Most of the classrooms in the building finally had air-conditioning (although the auditorium, the corridors, and some offices were as hot as ever). The city had finally fulfilled its promise to give the children of Brighter Choice an amenity that other schools had enjoyed for years.

Parents like Keesha who had kept their children home out of fear of COVID-19 began to send them back to class, impressed by the safety measures Mr. Daniel had put in place—and by his willingness to give individual tours to wary parents to show them what the classrooms were like. Every classroom had an air purifier. Children and teachers wore masks (except during lunch) and tables were spaced at least 3 feet apart. Attendance in September was still well below the pre-pandemic norm, but it was higher than it had been during the 2020–2021 school year. Every few days, a new child would return to class as parents became more confident of their safety.

A new assistant principal gave parents ever more confidence in the direction the school would take: Ms. Nunes, the award-winning 5th grade teacher, was promoted to the post that had been vacant for 2 years. She had just received a master's degree in administration from Bank Street College of Education, the same progressive school Ms. Fabayo and Mama Fela attended. Ms. Nunes had roots in the community: She had worked with Ms. Fabayo, Brighter Choice's founding principal, and had sent her own children to Little Sun People. Ms. Nunes's long teaching experience promised to give Mr. Daniel critical support in strengthening the quality of instruction.

Ms. Deittra, a passionate and effective advocate for the school, continued to offer frequent tours for prospective parents throughout the pandemic, moving them to Zoom when it was too dangerous to invite people in person. Her pitch attracts parents who share the school's commitment to racial justice, who are looking for a place where everyone feels part of a community—whether they live in a townhouse or a homeless shelter.

Her recruitment efforts and the school's growing reputation paid off: Even as public-school enrollments dropped across New York City during the pandemic, Brighter Choice held its own. Three quarters of New York City public schools had declining enrollments in 2021–2022; nearly one quarter declined by more than 10%, due to falling birth rates, the migration of families to the suburbs, and competition from charters and private schools (many of which had stayed open when public schools closed). (1) But at Brighter Choice, enrollment held steady at 302, just 5 fewer than the previous year. The school served a mix of students with different racial and economic backgrounds. In 2021–2022, about half of those enrolled were Black, 35% were Latino, and 15% were White, Asian, or multiracial.

New York City schools had an influx of cash, thanks to new promises from the federal and state governments. President Joe Biden, who took office on January 20, 2021, with slim Democratic majorities in the House and Senate, had passed a $1.9 trillion relief bill. The American Rescue Plan Act provided almost $125 billion for education. New York City's share of that money, $6.9 billion, amounted to $7,200 per pupil, to be spent over 3 years. In addition, the New York State Legislature agreed to fully fund a formula called Foundation Aid, the result of the 1993 lawsuit by the Campaign for Fiscal Equity (CFE) that argued the state was short-changing New York City. The city would get an additional $530 million from the state for the 2021–2022 school year. (2)

These new funds meant that Brighter Choice could devote more resources to helping children catch up from the ground they lost during the pandemic. In addition, Mr. Daniel planned one-on-one after-school tutoring and small group instruction for children who needed it.

On a personal note, Keesha's health was better. She had taken 6 months off work, which helped reduce her stress levels. By the time she returned to work, she had learned to cope better. She had been seeing a therapist and was getting more exercise and eating healthier meals. Her cardiologist said her condition had improved so much she no longer needed heart surgery.

The community held together through the darkest days of the pandemic. Faced with constant confusion from city, state, and federal officials about safety procedures, Mr. Daniel reassured parents that he had their backs. He shared his own fears. He promised teachers and staff he would never ask them to do something he wasn't willing to do himself.

At a time when trust was in short supply—when most teachers mistrusted the de Blasio administration and parents were confused by conflicting and ever-changing health guidelines from the state and federal government—Mr. Daniel had won over both staff and parents. "Trust is the glue," Mr. Daniel told me.

Building trusting relationships within a school not only fosters a sense of community, it is also a crucial key ingredient in improving children's academic performance. As researchers who tracked 12 Chicago elementary schools over a period of 10 years discovered, only those with an atmosphere of trust among parents, teachers, and administrators saw improvements in achievement. Schools with trusting relationships, the researchers found, are more likely to have other ingredients that foster student achievement. Teachers are more willing to innovate and to work together collectively. Parents are more engaged. And everyone is more likely to have a long-term commitment to the school, a stability that can help the school improve. (3)

The atmosphere at the school had changed markedly from 2018, Mr. Daniel's first year, when the PTA president was openly hostile to the new principal and there was friction within the parent body. Keesha, along with the other parents in the PTA and the SLT, created a climate in which parents could air their concerns about outdoor recess, or the quality of Spanish language instruction, or the school's test scores, but always in a respectful way, with the assumption that the administration would do its best to address their complaints.

Parents and staff worked to include everyone and took steps to make the lives of the school's most vulnerable children a little easier. One Saturday in April 2021, fathers hauled a washer and dryer to the school; the machines had been donated by Ms. Cintron, the social worker, so that homeless families—or anyone else—could wash their clothes at Brighter Choice. Ibrahim, the leader of Fathers on a Mission, borrowed a truck. Mr. Daniel and Terrance Johnson, the father the kids called Coach TJ, picked up the appliances at Ms. Cintron's home and brought them to the school, where they left them in the PTA room.

The school organized activities to recognize the struggles of different racial and ethnic groups. On a beautiful, sunny Saturday in June, about 50 adults and children, including prospective families who were considering enrolling their children in the fall, gathered on the playground for an "anti-hate rally" and the school's "spring carnival." It was a multiracial group, mostly Black and Latino families but a few White and Asian ones as well.

Although rally in 2020 had focused on police brutality against Black Americans, the rally in 2021 also recognized anti-Asian violence. Xenophobic attacks on Asian Americans had been on the rise throughout the COVID-19 pandemic; innocent people were increasingly targeted, assaulted, and even killed, simply because the virus originated in China. The Brighter Choice community wanted to show support for all victims of hatred. Children held up cardboard signs with slogans of peace and racial unity: "Be Kind to Everyone!" "Stop Asian Hate!" "Black Lives Matter!" Mr. Daniel, wearing shorts and holding a bullhorn, led the crowd in a march around the block chanting:

"Two, four, six, eight! Stop the violence, stop the hate!"

Two weeks later, parents and children gathered for the last Skate Club of the year. It fell on June 19, also known as Juneteenth. Mr. Daniel gathered parents and children in a circle on the playground to say a few words about the holiday, which commemorates African Americans' emancipation from slavery. "The work is not done," he said. "There are forces then and now that want to get rid of people's rights."

The year before, when Brighter Choice parents and children staged a Black Lives Matter demonstration on Juneteenth, the holiday in New York City was celebrated mostly within the African American community. This year, the Department of Education had declared Juneteenth a school holiday, and President Biden had just signed legislation making it a federal holiday.

In the fall of 2021, parents organized events that brought together families from different backgrounds. New parents and old met once again at the Carousel in Prospect Park one Saturday in September and chatted while the children rode. Fathers on a Mission set up the annual "Take Your Child to School" breakfast, with tables outdoors to prevent the spread of COVID-19. Family Movie Night, too, was outdoors, with folding chairs and a movie screen put up on the playground.

On a Saturday in mid-October, the PTA organized a celebration of Hispanic Heritage Month, the first time it had organized an event especially honoring Latino culture. Flags of Mexico, Puerto Rico, and the countries of Central and South America were displayed on the fences around the playground. A boom box played Latin music and an instructor offered free flamenco lessons. Trays of empanadas, taquitos, arroz con leche, and other treats were spread out on folding tables. Ms. Deittra wrote signs with prices for the food as Keesha put out trays of sweet rolls.

Few Spanish-speaking parents had come to PTA events in the past, but many came to this one. Parents and children of all races and ethnicities enjoyed the food and joined in the dancing. I asked Jess, the only Spanish-speaking mother on the PTA board, what was different this time, why the Spanish-speaking parents had turned out in such numbers. The secret, she said, is to ask them to bring food.

"Food is so important to Latin American culture. They made all of this," she said, gesturing toward the tables laden with food.

If Spanish-speaking parents hadn't taken part in PTA events before, maybe it was because nobody had asked them. And if parents with limited English had been seen as people who needed help—such as translation services—this event focused on their strengths and the contributions they could make to the community. This approach—identifying and valuing the contributions that all parents can make—helped Brighter Choice engage Spanish-speaking parents. The same approach would enlist the help of another group that rarely came to the school: homeless parents. Mr. Daniel told me he was thrilled when several mothers in temporary housing agreed to chaperone a class trip to the aquarium.

"This year feels really different," Big Keyonn told me. "It's almost a rebirth. Everyone is committed to participating. There is an air of inclusivity, intentional inclusiveness."

The fall wasn't entirely a love fest of intergroup understanding, however. A dispute was brewing over the holiday show to be held at the school in December.

Two years before, the holiday show had been a big success—a multifaith, multicultural concert with songs from many traditions. No one seemed to mind whether the song their child sang matched the religion they practiced at home, perhaps because so many faiths were represented. But this year's show—a play called Winter Wonderland with a scene at Santa's Workshop at the North Pole—was, given the staff shortages in the wake of the pandemic, a much simpler affair. And, for some parents, the show seemed to be a Christmas celebration, not a multicultural one. A Muslim couple objected to the fact that their children were expected to sing "Santa Claus Is Coming to Town."

These parents, a Palestinian American mother and a Pakistani American father, saw themselves as members of both religious and racial minorities—not "White." At the same time, the mother, a hospital administrator, and her husband, an investment banker, were newcomers to a historically Black neighborhood with a higher income level than most of the other parents at Brighter Choice.

The Muslim parents—who asked me not to use their names—were told by their teacher that their children could sit out if they didn't want to participate. Frustrated by the response, they spoke with Mr. Daniel—whose wife was expecting a baby any day. Mr. Daniel consulted with the director of the after-school program (who had written the play and was organizing the rehearsals), but he didn't offer an immediate solution. The children had already started rehearsing and the after-school staff—who were putting on the show with a skeleton crew, thanks to the strain of the pandemic—was reluctant to change.

The parents raised their concerns on a WhatsApp chat group for Brighter Choice parents. Some fellow parents agreed the song was a problem: A few thought the line "He sees you when you're sleeping" was creepy, regardless of anyone's religious or cultural background. So, the parents in the chat group decided to bring up the issue at the PTA meeting the next day, November 18.

Keesha was taken aback when 40 parents showed up on the Zoom call that night—more than double the usual number. She had just learned about the Santa Claus debate and wasn't sure how to respond.

On the Zoom call, she moved through the regular PTA agenda. She introduced members of the PTA board, which had grown to 10 members, five Black and five White. She told parents about plans for the popcorn fundraiser, the middle school fair, and the "gift of giving" or holiday store set up for the children to choose gifts for their parents. She asked for donations for the bake sale for the holiday show.

When Keesha opened the floor to questions, one of the new board members, a Jewish father whose child was in 3K, raised the concerns of the WhatsApp group about the Santa Claus song. He said parents had originally been told their children would sing Winter Wonderland, a nondenominational song. For reasons that were not clear, the song had been changed to one about Santa Claus. A number of parents were reluctant to have their children sing a song grounded in a religious tradition—Christianity—and preferred to have them sing Winter Wonderland, as originally planned.

Keesha cut off the discussion. She said the PTA wasn't responsible for the holiday show. She advised parents to raise their concerns on another Zoom call the next day with Mr. Daniel and the staffer from the afterschool program who was putting on the show. Keesha, who felt she had done her part by directing parents to a forum where they could resolve the issue, adjourned the meeting.

The Muslim couple felt they were getting the runaround. They had raised their concerns with their children's teachers, with the principal, and with the PTA to no avail. The next morning, this mother sent an email to the school administration—a note that somehow began to circulate among parents. The email only served to compound the hurt feelings all around.

The mother had chosen Brighter Choice, she wrote, thinking it was a community that "appreciates and respects diversity, different points of view, thoughts, cultures, and religions." The PTA meeting, she said, "was the complete opposite."

She said, "not much has changed" in the 30 years since her family moved to the United States and her parents taught her to "assimilate and accept the status quo. . . . What environment are we fostering if we cannot respect other opinions and thoughts?"

Just about the same time the email went out, Mr. Daniel's wife went into labor. He accompanied her to the hospital, and then went home so he could join the Zoom call that afternoon with parents, including the Muslim couple, and the staffer from the after-school program. Worn out by the debate—but not understanding why it was such a big deal for some parents—Mr. Daniel directed the after-school program to drop Santa Claus from the show. He was back at the hospital in time to see his wife deliver a baby boy.

"Santa's Workshop" was renamed "Toy Workshop." The song about Santa Claus was removed. The parents who had made the complaint were satisfied. But Keesha and some of the other Black women in the PTA were bitter about the email the Palestinian mother had sent.

Keesha was infuriated by the accusation that the PTA had no respect for diversity or different points of view. After all, she had spent more than 2 years trying to build bridges among parents of different races and family incomes. She had defended Mr. Daniel when some Black parents turned against him. She had mediated disputes between White parents who wanted their children to go out for recess and Black and Latino families who wanted to keep children inside. She helped organize countless community-building events such as the Carousel, Hispanic Heritage Day, and Friendsgiving. How could someone accuse her of intolerance?

Particularly irksome, she told me, was what she thought was the email's suggestion that any slights Muslim parents may have endured 30 years ago were somehow comparable to the racism Black Americans endure today. Now, the email didn't say that—it only said that Muslim immigrant families a generation ago were expected to assimilate and accept the status quo—but, nonetheless, the email upset Keesha so much she almost quit the PTA.

"I was like, 'I'm done.' I can't go on like this. I can't, because it hurts," she told me several months later. "Every day on the news, I'm looking at, what child is being shot by the cops today? What manner of violence is happening to Black children? All right, you have to go 30 years to find the oppression for your parents. I have to wake up every day and deal with racism in

America. Fear of whether my son or husband, when they walk out the door, will they return?"

The Palestinian mother told me she never suggested her parents' experience as immigrants was in any way comparable to the oppression suffered by Black Americans. The email, she said, was simply meant to explain why she didn't want her children to sit out when other children sang the Santa Claus song—the alternative a teacher had suggested. "I did not want my children to be isolated from their peers due to their religious background," she told me. "This is unacceptable in a public-school setting."

She wasn't against holiday celebrations—her family happily went to see Christmas lights in the Italian American neighborhood of Dyker Heights. They had lit Chanukah candles with Jewish friends. But those were activities they chose as a family, not activities imposed by a public school that required members of religious minorities either to participate in a symbol of the dominant culture or face exclusion. She was happy to have her children learn *about* religion in school—say, the history of St. Nicholas—but in their eyes the Santa Claus show seemed to endorse one holiday.

Keesha never told the Palestinian mother how hurt she felt. Just before Christmas, Keesha contracted COVID-19 and was home sick for 3 weeks—and away from PTA business. Big Keyonn and Little Keyonn contracted COVID-19 as well, although their cases were mild compared to Keesha's.

By the middle of December, the highly contagious Omicron variant of COVID-19 was spreading, and even vaccinated people were getting sick. Mr. Daniel decided it was too risky to have the holiday show in person, so the children's performance was recorded and broadcast via Zoom. Any controversy over the content seemed moot, given the uneven quality of the recording, and the words of the songs were hard to hear. The holiday bake sale was canceled, as was the "gift of giving" where children chose presents to give their parents. Nearly 50 children and staff tested positive for COVID-19 in December and January; others had been exposed to the virus and had to quarantine. Some parents kept their children home out of fear of infection. By the week before Christmas, attendance had plummeted to 47%.

Whatever bad feelings remained after the Santa Claus debate didn't keep the parents of Brighter Choice from trying to work together. In the months after the show, the Muslim couple showed up for just about every event and every parent meeting on Zoom, as did the members of the PTA who had been there for years: Keesha, Jess, Brandi, Shayla, and Frances. "Building bridges and moving forward is the only option, for the sake of our community," the Palestinian mother told me.

On an unseasonably warm Saturday in mid-February, the families of Brighter Choice celebrated Black History Month with a buffet lunch on the playground. There were waffles and fried chicken from Cheri's Bedstuy, a soul food restaurant owned by one of the parents, Torri Clayton. There were Haitian specialties from another restaurant, Grandchamps, owned by Sabrina Brockman, the parent who served as head of the School Leadership Team. Children from a nearby middle school performed a dance. The rapper ELUCID, a father at the school, read a poem.

If the Santa Claus debate had exposed rifts in the community, the Black History celebration showed the strength the school draws from its neighborhood institutions—including the Black restaurateurs and entertainers of Bedford-Stuyvesant. The celebration also showed the potential for solidarity as families of different races and religions gathered on the playground. It was nice to see the Palestinian mother exchange hugs with Black friends.

The next PTA event on May 6 was a lunch for Teacher Appreciation Day. Keesha, who had to fight with her employer to get the day off, was mostly on her own to organize the celebration. Other parents sent food, but only one other mother was able to help Keesha set up in the school library. Jess, who was usually on hand to help, had a job she couldn't miss. Frances had planned to help but had to stay home when her daughter got sick. For some parents, this was a sign the PTA needed to expand its pool of volunteers and not rely exclusively on the PTA board.

"Keesha works so hard," Emily Schlesinger, a board member (and one of the Jewish parents who had backed the request to drop the Santa song), told me in a phone call. "She burned herself out and she kind of burned the board out, too." Certainly, by late spring the parents who were active in the PTA were worn out.

Emily taught at another school and could not attend events at Brighter Choice during the school day. But she was filled with ideas of ways the PTA could engage parents in the coming year—including those who were working during school hours—and be more efficient: send requests for volunteers to the whole parent body, not just the board members; sell school uniforms online, and not rely on parents to sell them in person at the school; arrange for online donations and payments by PayPal or Venmo, rather than cash. As the school attracted more middle-class and professional parents, there was the potential to make the PTA a more effective operation and to share the burden of fundraising and organizing activities across a larger group of parents.

At Saturday Skate Club on May 14, I met another mother, Arissa Hall, who planned to run for PTA president in June when Keesha's term expired. A Black community organizer who leads a nonprofit called S.O.U.L. Sisters Leadership Collective, Arissa had significant professional experience managing budgets, writing grants, and building an organization. She agreed with Emily that much could be done to improve communication, to engage more parents, and to adopt up-to-date banking and budgeting systems. One of her key goals was to boost the school's enrollment by finding ways to encourage parents who withdrew their children from Brighter Choice after prekindergarten to stay.

I asked her about the disputes that seemed to fall along race and class lines, like the Santa Claus debate. She said debate is healthy, and voicing disagreements is necessary to resolving differences.

"I don't think conflict is a bad thing," she said. "I think if we're not having conflict, something's wrong. Conflict exposes the differences or the challenges. How do we move through that together? What are the methods to move to that?"

Working through the challenges, she said, was possible at a place like Brighter Choice, where parents of different races and income levels had a shared interest in ensuring their children had a good education. At the same time, it's impossible to ignore the history and current state of racial inequality.

"I don't think we'll ever have some 'We Are the World,' 'Kumbaya,' multiracial dream if we are not honest about what got us here, which is a very real racialized system that we live in, that continues to oppress Black people at this moment," she said.

Shortly after we left the playground, horrifying news spread: An 18-year-old White supremacist shot and killed ten Black people in a Buffalo supermarket, 370 miles northwest of New York City, in a sickening act of domestic terrorism. Dealing with the fear and anger over the killings would be another challenge for the Brighter Choice community.

When children returned to school Monday morning, Mr. Daniel gathered them on the playground for "Community Circle," the weekly assemblies where he shared news and announcements. In the first circle for the smallest children, Mr. Daniel made no mention of the massacre but reminded the children that they must be kind to one another. At the second circle for the older children, he was a little more direct, saying horrible, hateful things had happened at a supermarket in Buffalo. Without mentioning the killings explicitly, he told the children it was their obligation to call out racism whenever they encountered it.

He sent an email to parents that night. "As principal of Brighter Choice Community School, I promise to never shy away from discussions about race, racism, and implicit bias and I recognize the importance of this work in a country that still has such a long way to go with reckoning with its racist past and horrific treatment of people of color."

Later that week, rumors spread among parents that there had been a racist incident at Brighter Choice. Mr. Daniel summoned parents to what he called an "emergency town hall," on Friday evening, May 20. Some 60 parents attended the Zoom call.

Mr. Daniel told parents that a 4th-grade girl, on two occasions, had said to another child, "I hate Blacks." Given the events in Buffalo, parents were alarmed. Mr. Daniel said he and the guidance counselor had both spoken to the girl, explaining that such talk was unacceptable. "Our goal as educators is to get to the root of it, and to find out why the child would feel the need to say that," he said. The girl told the guidance counselor that another child had picked on her; the guidance counselor, who is Black, said, it's important not to say hateful things about a whole group of people. The girl seemed to understand.

Some parents were satisfied that the school had handled the situation well; others would have preferred a more punitive approach, such as suspending the girl. All the parents were glad that Mr. Daniel had been forthcoming about the situation.

In my years visiting the school, I did hear of a few other cases in which small children made racially tinged comments. A few years before, a White boy told a Black classmate, "I am White, and a long time ago I would have owned you"—a clumsy reference to his newfound recognition of racial differences and the history of slavery. Also a few years before, another White boy said to a Black classmate: "You came from monkeys." In his mind, his mother told me, he was making a reference to evolution and the fact that we are all descended from primates, but it was a mortifying comment, whatever he was thinking. I heard about those cases directly from the parents involved; the case of the girl saying "I hate Blacks" was the first time the whole Brighter Choice community learned of such a comment.

Mr. Daniel took care not to identify the girl, to protect her privacy. But I later learned that both the girl who said "I hate Blacks" and the boy she said it to were Latino. The boy was darker-skinned than the girl, but the incident was not, as many parents had assumed, a case of a White perpetrator and a Black victim.

As a fuller picture of the episode emerged, the girl's circumstances also suggested she was a victim as well as a perpetrator. She was new to the school, had lost her housing, and was living with her mother and a sibling in a homeless shelter. At Brighter Choice, she had been assigned to a special education class and seemed to have been traumatized—by whom it wasn't clear—and the school was working hard to help her with her difficulties.

Mr. Daniel told me later he was satisfied that the school's approach was effective and appropriate, and the girl seemed to be adjusting well. "She was very remorseful," Mr. Daniel said. "On Saturday she was at Skate Club, skating with kids of every color."

TEN

The Work Still to Be Done

Kristina Bumphrey? Kristina B. Photography

Parents work for the common good, not just what will benefit their own children.

Arissa organized a Zoom call with 3K and pre-K parents to address a troubling pattern: middle-class and professional parents, particularly White but also Black, often withdraw their children from Brighter Choice after prekindergarten. This creates a division in the school between the "early childhood" classes, which are mixed by race and income, and the older grades, which have fewer White and more low-income students. Just as important, attrition has an impact on the budget, because the school receives money according to the number of children enrolled.

At Brighter Choice, the classes for 3- and 4-year-olds were oversubscribed, with long wait lists. The upper grades had room to spare.

Arissa reasoned that giving parents a forum to speak out might give the administration the tools it needed to address their concerns. Mr. Daniel, Ms. Nunes, Ms. Deittra, and a few teachers agreed to take part in what they called a "listening session" on Zoom the evening of May 24. Arissa asked the two dozen parents present on the call to recount the school's "strengths" and "opportunities." Most pointedly she asked: What do you need to keep your child enrolled through 5th grade?

Every parent who spoke praised the school's sense of community, the teachers' dedication, and the responsiveness of the administration. They all felt welcome at the school. But a few were also worried that the academics weren't challenging, particularly for older children. One mother who spoke Spanish at home said she was disappointed with the dual-language prekindergarten class: Her son not only had not learned Spanish in class, he had actually forgotten the Spanish he knew. Several Black parents said the school needed to better address different skills levels among children with more small group instruction (rather than having the teacher speak to the whole class). A White mother suggested the school might adopt interdisciplinary projects—such as a year-long study of oceans she'd heard about at another school. (The school had such projects under Ms. Fabayo's leadership, but not in recent years.) Most of the parents who spoke were committed to staying at Brighter Choice, but a few seemed to be on the fence.

Over the 3 years I spent visiting Brighter Choice, parents consistently praised the warmth of the community, but it wasn't always enough to keep them at the school. Attrition is inevitable, of course. Some parents, White and Black, left for suburban homes when they outgrew their small city apartments. Some African American parents moved to the South—part of a trend that is beginning to reverse the Great Migration that brought

Keesha's parents to Brooklyn. Other parents may have never intended to keep their children at Brighter Choice beyond the early childhood years: They wanted a competitive, very fast-paced school culture that Brighter Choice, with its inclusive values, did not offer. But this doesn't explain all parents' decisions to leave. Even some parents who seemed committed to Brighter Choice's values left. Their choices help explain why it is so difficult to attract and retain families at high-poverty schools.

Virginia, the White mother who was part of the Bed-Stuy Parents Committee and who joined the school in Mr. Daniel's first year, complained that her 4-year-old was expected to sit still for long periods of time, watching videos on the classroom Smart Board. She transferred her son to a progressive charter school for kindergarten.

Lauren and Talia, White mothers who had been active in the PTA, kept their children at Brighter Choice for 1st grade even as other White families withdrew their children. Then they, too, became disenchanted, saying instruction was moving at a glacial pace. They transferred their children to PS 9, a popular, racially mixed neighborhood school with a progressive curriculum in the adjoining District 13.

Kamilah Duggins, an African American mother who was active in the PTA, withdrew her daughter in 2021 after 3rd grade, disappointed that the school never fulfilled its promise of a project-based curriculum, she told me. There were too many worksheets, not enough movement in class, and not enough time spent reading whole books, creating artwork, or playing outside. She transferred her child to Academy of Arts & Letters, a progressive public school of choice in District 13. Significantly, each of these parents sought out racially mixed schools with mixed-ability classrooms—not majority-White schools or "gifted" programs. But the schools they chose also had a higher proportion of middle-class children than Brighter Choice has.

Lauren and Talia withdrew their children in the darkest days of the pandemic, when teachers were improvising online lessons; Kamilah left after the year of "hybrid" classes, when there were many disruptions because of COVID-19. It may not have been a fair time, in either case, to judge a school's effectiveness. However, their complaints highlight some of the difficulties that high-poverty schools face as they work to offer a demanding academic program.

A school like Brighter Choice, founded on progressive principles, is caught between some parents' demands for a creative and challenging curriculum and the bureaucratic imperative, in an era of standards-based education, to raise test scores—even if the tests only measure low-level skills.

Middle-class and professional parents, who have the luxury of many school options, tend to seek out schools where children learn to think for themselves, where they have class discussions, where they write essays rather than fill in worksheets—giving them the skills and habits that will prepare them for college and professional life. They are less likely to worry about standardized tests: They are confident their children will score well because of the advantages they have at home and, in any case, they have resources for tutoring and private test prep outside of school if their children need it.

On the other hand, teachers and administrators at high-poverty schools are under tremendous pressure to boost test scores, particularly for the weakest students. The open-ended approach to learning that many better-off parents prefer is less likely to raise a school's test scores, at least in the short-term, than the traditional, scripted curriculum with worksheets and test prep based on reading short passages.

Partly as a result of this pressure, partly because of teachers' inexperience or preference, high-poverty schools tend to have a curriculum that focuses on basic skills, in which the teacher does most of the talking and children sit quietly, filling out worksheets at their desks. Recent research shows kindergartners in high-poverty schools spend more time in "whole class instruction"—that is, listening to the teacher—rather than working in small groups. They have less opportunity to choose their own activities; they spend less time on physical exercise and more time waiting in line than children in low-poverty schools. (1) Low-income children, on average, hear fewer challenging words from their teachers and have access to fewer classroom books than children in more prosperous communities. (2)

Competing demands—for higher test scores on the one hand and a more creative approach to learning on the other—highlight the debate between traditional and progressive education that has been raging for more than 100 years. Is it more important for children to learn the basic skills that traditional schools stress—spelling and punctuation and the multiplication tables? Or is it more important, as progressive educators argue, for children to learn how to gather information rather than memorize facts?

The debate often takes on a racial dimension, as education researcher Lisa Delpit has noted. Delpit, who is African American, was teaching in a racially integrated school in Philadelphia in the 1970s when she set up a progressive classroom—with cozy rugs instead of desks, and "stations" or centers where children could move around to choose different activities. She offered math games, fun-to-read books, and a creative writing program. She discovered, to her dismay, that well-to-do White children zoomed ahead while lower-income Black children in the same classroom threw books and practiced karate moves because they were not accustomed to an unstructured classroom.

As Delpit became a more experienced teacher, she began to incorporate more explicit instruction and "traditional" practices, such as handwriting practice, and her lower-income Black students' performance improved. But she didn't limit her teaching to basic skills. She says children are shortchanged in traditional classrooms that *only* offer meaningless and repetitive drills—as classrooms serving mostly Black children often do. Children who only master low-level skills, who don't learn to think critically and creatively, receive an education that only prepares them for low-level jobs, and, just as important, fails to prepare them for the demands of citizenship such as voting, jury duty, and other civic responsibilities. Schools need to offer *both* basic skills *and* the opportunity for creative thinking. But it's a devilishly difficult task. (3)

The staff of Brighter Choice has been navigating these issues since its founding. Under Ms. Fabayo's leadership, the school worked to offer children both traditional skills and creative lessons. For example, she used the structured Open Court reading program, with its emphasis on phonics, as well as the Teachers College writing program, which encourages children to develop their own voice. The school had an interdisciplinary social studies curriculum, where children would study topics such as "transportation," or "family," or "Native Americans."

By the time Mr. Daniel became principal, most of the founding teachers of Brighter School were gone, and the new teachers used a variety of techniques. The school continued to offer children hands-on activities—planting vegetables in the school garden, cooking the vegetables they grow, practicing African dance and drumming, and learning the principles of flight by making paper airplanes. At the same time, the academic program was more traditional than it had been before Brighter Choice merged with Young Scholars.

Mr. Daniel chose a reading program, HMH Into Reading, because it offered texts in both English and Spanish—important for the school's dual-language program. The program focuses on reading short passages and answering questions from a textbook, rather than whole books you might read for pleasure. It is a program designed to prepare children for the brief texts and multiple-choice questions they face on standardized tests. Some parents have complained the scripted program is boring, with little opportunity for strong readers to move ahead and for slower readers to get extra help—and little opportunity to develop a love of reading.

The best teachers at Brighter Choice, confident in their abilities, create their own lessons to supplement the reading program. They give children complete books to read, in addition to the short passages in the textbooks. They know how to "differentiate instruction," that is, challenge top students while giving others the support they need. But other teachers rely on the scripted lessons.

The pandemic increased the urgency of finding ways to teach children with a range of skills in the same class. When children returned to class full-time in the fall of 2021, some had been able to keep up with their studies, thanks to parents with the resources to supervise their lessons home (or even hire private tutors), while others had fallen seriously behind.

The gaps between the haves and have-nots were as wide as ever, but the staff at Brighter Choice rallied with what science teacher Wilma Ambrose called "all hands on deck." All adults in the building were enlisted to bolster children's skills. The science teacher and even the gym teacher incorporated reading and writing into their lessons. The school used federal money from the American Rescue Plan to offer small-group instruction and tutoring after school and on Saturdays. A newly hired "literacy coach" worked with teachers to develop strategies for struggling readers.

As assistant principal, Ms. Nunes worked closely with teachers to help them perfect their craft, drawing on her many years' experience as a classroom teacher. Her approach is collegial, and she praises teachers for their strengths while making suggestions for improvements. She makes sure teachers have the books and supplies they need, including "class sets" of novels and nonfiction books, so teachers don't rely exclusively on the short passages in the reading textbooks. At the "listening session" Arissa organized on Zoom, Ms. Nunes reassured parents that every class, from pre-K to 5th grade, has "small group instruction," a way to ensure that strong students are challenged and weaker students get the support they need.

Mr. Daniel, ever responsive to parents' concerns about their children sitting still in class, made outdoor recess a priority and organized time for children to play outside before school. Some classrooms got beanbag chairs so children could move from their desks when they were fidgety. Mr. Daniel also worked to accommodate children who needed more academic challenges. For example, a 1st-grader who had mastered 1st-grade math was allowed to attend math lessons with 2nd-graders. At the "listening session," Mr. Daniel said he welcomed parents' ideas and would work with them in the coming year to implement many of them.

These efforts seemed to be bearing fruit, both strengthening the quality of teaching and improving retention. Increasingly, middle-income families, particularly Black families, were keeping their children at Brighter Choice. In 2018, 85% of children were poor enough to qualify for free lunch; by 2022 just 62% were. When Mr. Daniel became principal, middle-income children were concentrated in prekindergarten; by 2022, there were middle-income children in all the grades. Racial diversity came more slowly. Most of the White children were clustered in 3K and pre-K. But here, too, the school was changing. While there were no White children in grades 4 and 5, there were a dozen White children in kindergarten through grade 3.

Parents were keeping their children at Brighter Choice even when they had alternatives. Jess, a Spanish-speaking White mother on the board of the PTA, turned down a "gifted" program at another school for her older son and kept both her boys at Brighter Choice. Alie Stumpf, a White mother who teaches at a public middle school in Manhattan, transferred her daughter *out* of a mostly White gifted program and into Brighter Choice. There was unhealthy competition at the gifted program, she said, and she valued the sense of community at Brighter Choice.

The parents who stay share some of the concerns of those who leave. But they say the school has rare strengths that outweigh any drawbacks.

"I love the community and my child is happy," said Brooke Vermillion, a White mother of a boy, Dion, who started at the school in 3K and was in 1st grade in 2021–2022. "I can't imagine pulling him out and taking him to another school and having him make new friends. He's just really thrived there and at the end of the day that's all that matters to me."

Brooke has found a way to deal with any difficulties her son faces without making a fuss. For example, she doesn't believe in homework for 1st-graders and often "forgets" to have her son Dion complete the worksheets sent home. And, while his teacher says he has trouble sitting still in class, Brooke found a way to make Dion less restless, by withdrawing him from the after-school program. She and another family hired a babysitter to take their children outside to play for 2½ hours after school. A shorter school day makes it easier for Dion to focus in class.

Frances, a Black mother who attended parochial school as a child, prefers a more traditional approach—and more homework—than Brighter Choice offers. To fill any gaps, she hired a private tutor to work with her 3rd-grade daughter, Aissa. She has her daughter practice handwriting at home. Still, Frances is a big fan of the school. She says building character and teaching children to be moral human beings is even more important than academics—and that makes Brighter Choice a perfect school for Aissa.

Brighter Choice, she says, teaches children to be fair and kind to one another. It gives them tools to fight for social justice—whether at Black Lives Matter demonstrations or in Ms. Ambrose's Sustainability Club, where children learn to recycle, save electricity, and prepare food packages for children in need. "It's your job to see where something is not right. Maybe you can make it better, or make it right," Frances told me.

When Shayla, a Black mother and speech therapist who attended private school as a child, enrolled her son in pre-K, she had low expectations and was braced to pull him out at any time. She has been pleasantly surprised by the quality of teaching and, now that her son is in 1st grade, she plans to stay. She believes that the upper grades will get stronger as more middle-income families keep their children in the school. "The parents will be more demanding, and that might make a difference," she said.

For many Black parents, the school's racial makeup is a plus. The school was 48% Black, 35% Hispanic, and just under 10% White, with a handful of Asian and multiracial children, in 2021–2022. For Sabrina, head of the School Leadership Team, it's important for her mixed-race children to be around other Black children. Ms. Deittra, another Black woman married to a White man, agrees. "I was so captivated by a really rich school that was predominantly Black and Brown," Ms. Deittra said, adding that she also values the fact that her son has classmates from families with different income levels.

"I want him to understand that the kids that he's sitting next to have different experiences, that no person is lesser in his eyes, because we're all in it together," she said. Emily, a White mother married to a Black man, said her family didn't want an all-White school, but didn't want an all-Black school either.

Some Black parents fear the school's demographics will change significantly as the neighborhood changes, as elderly Black homeowners leave, more young White families move in, and housing prices skyrocket. The fact that the school is surrounded by large public housing developments means that some low-income Black and Latino families will continue to live in the neighborhood, even as new construction offers new apartments for higher income families. Since any child who lives in the school's attendance zone is guaranteed a seat in the school, it's unlikely that low-income children will be forced out even if Brighter Choice, which still has empty classrooms, increases its enrollment. Still, the changes in the neighborhood are undeniable. When low-income families move out of the neighborhood, they are replaced by people with higher incomes.

Whatever their fears of the future, the founding principal, Ms. Fabayo, the current principal, Mr. Daniel, the staff, and parents at Brighter Choice have achieved something remarkable. In a beleaguered district where parents have avoided their local schools for decades, they built a sought-after school that even attracts families from outside the immediate neighborhood. In a city where parents tend to look at one another as competitors for scarce resources—that is, seats in a "good" school—Brighter Choice has created a community of shared interests, where parents work together to create better opportunities for all children. In a racially segregated city, Brighter Choice has created an integrated school.

Brighter Choice is still a school that honors African American culture, and, as Keesha had promised in her first PTA meeting nearly 3 years before, it has grown to incorporate other cultures as well. It values the contributions of all parents—such as the mothers in temporary housing who chaperoned a field trip to the aquarium—not just those who can raise money for the school.

During Keesha's tenure as PTA president, not every attempt at intergroup understanding was a success. Some disputes seemed to be resolved, only to reappear, like the ongoing debate over outdoor recess. Some quarrels left a bad taste in everyone's mouth, like Talia and Keesha's dispute over who would set up Movie Night. Some things that were important to one group seemed trivial to another—like the Santa Claus debate.

But the parents of Brighter Choice are clearly trying to learn from one another. They did a good job restoring trust in the PTA after $7,000 disappeared. Saturday Skate Club was a chance to meet informally on the playground. The School Leadership Team and PTA meetings were forums to air grievances and propose solutions. The Hispanic Heritage Celebration recognized the contributions of Spanish-speaking parents. These efforts count for a lot. Just as important, the children of Brighter Choice are growing up seeing that it's perfectly normal to go to school with children who are different from them.

The PTA elections on June 2, conducted on a Zoom call, brought some energetic new parents to the PTA board: Arissa was elected as the new president. The Muslim mother at the center of the Santa Claus debate became vice president of early childhood. Jess, Shayla, and Keesha remained on the board as vice presidents for the coming year. Emily became the recording secretary. No one wanted to be treasurer—a particularly thankless job that they would try to fill in the fall. Still, the PTA board had a solid core of parents—three of whom were Black, one was Muslim, one was Jewish, and one was Spanish-speaking—and seemed to be on more solid footing than it had been when Keesha became president 3 years before.

Keesha told me she had succeeded in her primary goal: to leave the PTA in a better place than she found it. She inherited a $10,000 deficit and left the PTA budget with a small surplus. She took over the PTA at a time when many of the lower-income families feared they would be displaced by higher-income newcomers; she succeeded in reassuring the long-time residents that they still mattered while enlisting the help of the newcomers. Like Arissa and Mr. Daniel, she believed conflict was inevitable and even healthy. "I don't think you should be afraid of conflict," she said. "Conflict brings about change, sometimes necessary change." At the same time, she was hopeful for the future.

"I know it is lofty and overly optimistic, to be aspiring for harmony and peace," Keesha said. "We're trying to get to the place where all of us can share the space. We need to be able to take new neighbors and old neighbors and share the space. I think our school has the ability to do that. I'm excited for next year."

Conclusion

Brighter Choice managed to foster a sense of trust at a time of dramatic change, conflict, and tension in the school and in the city. Brighter Choice held its own even as tens of thousands of families left the city during the pandemic and the number of students enrolled in the New York City public schools declined by more than 8%. (1) Brighter Choice may be a tiny school in the gigantic New York City school system, serving just 300 of the city's 1 million students. But the lessons it has to teach reverberate beyond its walls.

Key to Brighter Choice's success are the Black parents who form the core of the PTA. Some of these parents attended private schools or mostly White public schools themselves and wanted something different for their own children: a school, in their own neighborhood, where Black and Brown children did not feel isolated, where all children learned tolerance and mutual understanding. Few of these parents had racial integration as a goal—they simply wanted a school that would nurture their children. But the school became more racially integrated as Latino, White, Asian, and multiracial families, attracted by the school's warm sense of community and its commitment to social justice, began to enroll their children. If integration in the 1960s typically meant busing Black children to predominantly White schools, integration at Brighter Choice today means White parents and children are learning what it means to be in the minority, Black parents are learning to lead multiracial coalitions, and people from all groups are learning to accommodate one another.

Brighter Choice is a work in progress. Chronic absenteeism is still high; academic achievement, as measured by test scores, is uneven. Nonetheless, the school is moving in the right direction. The extraordinary dedication of the principal and staff—who frequently work on Saturdays and are always accessible to parents—coupled with parents' eagerness to be involved has produced an atmosphere of mutual trust. Parents frequently voice their concerns, but in a way that's supportive, not critical, and that is respectful of the principal and the teachers' authority. Most of all, parents are willing to work for common good, not just for their own children.

The children mostly get along. In my 3 years observing the school, I did hear of a few cases in which children made cringeworthy, racially tinged comments. Many parents were alarmed when a Latina girl said "I hate Blacks" to a darker skinned classmate. But the school administration is not afraid to confront issues of race openly and directly, whether in a "town hall" meeting, a Black Lives Matter demonstration, a celebration of Hispanic Heritage, or a debate over a Christmas song that Muslim parents felt excluded them.

The changing demographics of Bedford-Stuyvesant make it possible to mix children of different races and family incomes without sending children long distances to school. That's not always possible to do. As income inequality has grown in the United States, rich people increasingly live in neighborhoods with other rich people, poor people in neighborhoods with other poor people. Many neighborhoods in New York are racially and economically segregated and schools reflect this, with a high concentration of low-income Black and Latino children in many, and, in a few, a high concentration of high-income White children. Even in the city's racially and economically integrated neighborhoods, schools often remain segregated.

But the city is changing, and, particularly at the elementary school level, a growing number of formerly high-poverty schools, like Brighter Choice, now serve a mix of children of different family incomes as well as different races and ethnicities. I led a team of researchers at InsideSchools.org that visited 80 such schools (about 10% of the city's elementary schools) and we discovered they have many features in common: an effective principal who is not afraid to welcome often-demanding middle-class families, teachers who adopt a challenging project-based curriculum (rather than the scripted lessons so common at high-poverty schools), and parents who put in the hard work to build a community where all children, regardless of race or economic status, feel they belong. Dual-language programs, where children have alternating lessons in English and Spanish, are another way to attract families from different backgrounds and income levels. Like other successful, economically mixed schools, Brighter Choice also has these features. (2)

Decades of research have demonstrated that socioeconomic integration—that is, mixing children of different family incomes, as Brighter Choice has done—offers one of the best hopes for improving school achievement for children from low-income families. Indeed, students from low-income families in economically diverse schools are as much as 2 years ahead of students from low-income families in high-poverty schools. (3) One reason poor White and Asian children tend to do better in school than poor Black and Latino children is that poor White and Asian children tend to have middle-income classmates, while poor Black and Latino children tend to go to school with other low-income children. In New York City, two thirds of Black and Latino children attend schools that have poverty rates of more than 75%. Only 21% of White children and 41% of Asian children attend schools with poverty rates that high. (4) Reducing high concentrations of poverty in schools offers the possibility of better academic outcomes for all children.

The best way to reduce high concentrations of poverty, of course, would be to reduce poverty overall. Harvard economist Raj Chetty is just one of dozens of researchers who have found that increasing the income of poor parents (with low-income tax credits or cash allowances) results in improved academic achievement for their children. Parents with higher incomes have less stress, more time to spend with their children, and more money for books and school supplies. It's not surprising that children do better in school when their families have more money. (5)

Sadly, our country seems to be resigned to both high levels of child poverty and the highest income inequality in the industrial world. During President Joe Biden's first year in office, there was a brief attempt to address child poverty with expansion of the Child Tax Credit—sending monthly payments of $250 to $300 per child to most American families—but Congress allowed the tax credit to expire at the end of 2021. In the absence of political will to deal with inequality or child poverty overall, socioeconomic integration of schools can at least begin to help boost low-income Black and Latino children's chances of academic success.

Socioeconomic integration—and the racial integration that often goes along with it—can benefit middle-class and professional White and Asian families as well. These families often stretch their budgets to buy overpriced housing in "good"—that is, very expensive—school districts with high local taxes (and overwhelmingly White and Asian enrollments). One study found that houses in zip codes with elementary schools with higher-than-average test scores cost 77% more than those in areas without—a difference that researcher Heather McGhee calls "a tax levied by racism that not everyone can afford." She says many families "feel like they're in an arms race, fleeing what racism has wrought on public education, with the average person being priced out of the competition." (6) By sending their children to a school like Brighter Choice—and investing their time and energy to make it strong—parents can take advantage of housing costs that, while increasing, are still lower than the most expensive suburbs.

The big question, of course, is whether the demographics of Brighter Choice—and Bedford-Stuyvesant—are stable. In Brooklyn, some schools that were once racially and economically mixed have "tipped" and now serve mostly White, higher-income families, the result of rising housing prices and the increased popularity of the schools. I don't think that's likely at Brighter Choice for a number of reasons. Brighter Choice is both a zoned neighborhood school and a school that accepts children outside its attendance zone. Unlike charter schools or other schools of choice (which don't admit children according to their home address), children who live in the attendance zone are guaranteed a seat, beginning in kindergarten. This means Brighter Choice is likely to serve children who live in modest apartment buildings and public housing developments, as well as those in nearby homeless shelters, for the foreseeable future. The more prosperous families at Brighter Choice mostly live outside the attendance zone. Should the school ever become overcrowded, those children are not guaranteed a seat. For now, enrollment at Brighter Choice is barely half of the building's capacity. While there are waitlists for the 3K and pre-K classes—with enrollments capped by the district office—all other grades have room to grow.

Brighter Choice has reconciled two strains of thought within the African American community: on the one hand, the belief that all-Black schools with Black teachers offer a much-needed refuge from racism and, on the other hand, the belief that integrated schools provide equity and prepare children for life in a multiracial democracy. Brighter Choice manages to accomplish the goals of both advocates of Black self-determination and integrationists. Founded as an Afrocentric school, Brighter Choice has learned to welcome Latino, White, and Asian children while maintaining its role as a place that nurtures Black children and affirms their history and culture.

School choice in New York City has long pitted families of different races and income levels against one another as parents scramble to enroll their children in "good" schools—usually defined as schools with high test scores. Brighter Choice has changed the definition of a "good" school and, in doing so, has allowed parents of different races and income levels to see they have a shared interest in building an effective school. Brighter Choice, while facing many challenges, holds the promise of teaching the tolerance and respect we need to bring together our fractious, multiethnic society. Brighter Choice is well on its way to building a just school in an unequal city.

Acknowledgments

Thanks to the parents and staff of Brighter Choice Community School, especially Keesha Wright-Sheppard and Jeremy Daniel, who let me follow them over 3 turbulent years.

Thanks to the Russell Sage Foundation, led by Sheldon Danziger, which gave me a grant to support my work, an office to work in, and, most of all, colleagues with whom I was able to share ideas as a visiting journalist in the fall of 2021. Special thanks to Galo Falchettore at Russell Sage, who analyzed data and made the maps for this book, and my fellow fellows Samuel Myers, Jr., Steven O. Roberts, John Bound, and Arline Geronimus, who helped me wrestle with the complex ideas in this book.

Thanks to the staff of Teachers College Press, especially Brian Ellerbeck, who has guided my work and encouraged me for decades.

Thanks to Mark Winston Griffin and Max Freeman, whose School Colors podcast provided critical source material on District 16 schools.

Special thanks to Brighter Choice parent Sabrina Brockman, my friends Jacquie Holland and Peter Eisenstadt, and my sister Lowry Hemphill, all of whom read drafts of the manuscript and offered valuable suggestions.

Most of all, thanks to my husband Robert Snyder, my COVID-19 companion and at-home editor extraordinaire, who provided the love and support I needed to complete this book. He cheered me on when my energy flagged, read and edited multiple drafts, and believed in me when I didn't believe in myself. Without him, this book never would have been written.

Notes

Chapter 1: A Proudly Black School in a Gentrifying Neighborhood

1. Michael Woodsworth, *Battle for Bed-Stuy: The Long War on Poverty in New York City* (Cambridge: Harvard University Press, 2016), 60.

2. Mark Winston Griffith and Max Freedman, "Episode 4: Agitate, Educate, Organize," School Colors (podcast), Oct. 11, 2019, https://www.schoolcolorspodcast.com/episodes/episode-4-agitate-educate-organize

3. Nicole Mader and Clara Hemphill, *The Paradox of Choice: How School Choice Divides New York City Elementary Schools* (New York: Center for New York City Affairs, 2018), 19, http://www.centernyc.org/the-paradox-of-choice

Chapter 2: The Roots of Inequality and the Struggle for Just Schools

1. Richard Rothstein, *The Color of Law: A Forgotten History of How Our Government Segregated America* (New York: Liveright Publishing Corporation, 2017).

2. Martha Biondi, *To Stand and Fight: The Struggle for Civil Rights in Postwar New York City* (Cambridge: Harvard University Press, 2006), 234–235; Craig Steven Wilder, *A Covenant with Color: Race and Social Power in Brooklyn* (New York: Columbia University Press, 2000), 193.

3. Brad Plumer and Nadja Popovich, "How Decades of Racist Housing Policy Left Neighborhoods Sweltering," *The New York Times*, Aug. 24, 2020, https://www.nytimes.com/interactive/2020/08/24/climate/racism-redlining-cities-global-warming.html; Jason Richardson et al., "Redlining and Neighborhood Health," *National Community Reinvestment Coalition*, Oct. 20, 2020, https://ncrc.org/holc-health/

4. Rothstein, 69.

5. Brian Purnell, *Fighting Jim Crow in the County of Kings: The Congress of Racial Equality in Brooklyn* (Lexington: University Press of Kentucky, 2013), 22, 66.

6. Purnell, 134–152.

7. Clarence Taylor, *Knocking at Our Own Door: Milton A. Galamison and the Struggle to Integrate New York City Schools* (Lanham: Lexington Books, 2001), 52.

8. George N. Allen, *Undercover Teacher* (Garden City: Doubleday, 1960).

9. Peter Golenbock, *In the Country of Brooklyn: Inspiration to the World* (New York: William Morrow, 2008), 146.

10. Wilder, 213.

11. Wilder, 220; Taylor, 141–142.

12. Peter Eisenstadt, *Rochdale Village: Robert Moses, 6,000 families, and New York City's Great Experiment in Integrated Housing* (Ithaca: Cornell University Press, 2010), 158.

13. Matthew F. Delmont, *Why Busing Failed: Race, Media and the National Resistance to School Segregation* (Oakland: University of California Press, 2016), 23–26.

14. Mark Winston Griffith, "Episode 2: Power to the People," School Colors (podcast), Sept. 19, 2019, https://www.schoolcolorspodcast.com/episodes/episode-2-power-to-the-people

15. Heather Lewis, *New York City Public Schools from Brownsville to Bloomberg: Community Control and its Legacy* (New York: Teachers College Press, 2013), 27; Jerald E. Podair, "'White' Values, 'Black' Values: The Ocean Hill–Brownsville Controversy and New York City Culture, 1965–1975," *Radical History Review*, 59:36–59, 1995, 51.

16. Jerald E. Podair, *The Strike That Changed New York: Blacks, Whites and the Ocean Hill–Brownsville Crisis* (New Haven: Yale University Press 2002), 214.

17. The New York Federal Reserve Board, *New York City School Spending Per Student*, 2012, https://www.newyorkfed.org/data-and-statistics/data-visualization/nyc-school-spending#interactive/table

18. The Editorial Board, "The Cities We Need," *The New York Times*, May 11, 2020, https://www.nytimes.com/2020/05/11/opinion/sunday/coronavirus-us-cities-inequality.html

Chapter 3: The Deep Decline and Uneven Revival of the City's Schools

1. Edward B. Fiske, "New York Crisis Forcing Schools to Stress the 3 R's," *New York Times*, June 22, 1976, https://www.nytimes.com/1976/06/22/archives/new-york-crisis-forcing-schools-to-stress-the-3-rs-schools-pushing.html

2. Joseph Viteritti, *Across the River: Politics and Education in the City* (New York: Holmes & Meier Publishers, Inc., 1983), 47.

3. Leonard Buder, "New York City Schools Weather Fiscal Crisis," *New York Times*, June 21, 1976, https://www.nytimes.com/1976/06/21/archives/new-york-city-schools-weather-fiscal-crisis.html

4. William Julius Wilson, *The Truly Disadvantaged: The Inner City, the Underclass, and Public Policy* (Chicago: University of Chicago Press, 1987).

5. Samuel G. Freedman, *Small Victories: The Real World of a Teacher, Her Students, and Their High School* (New York: Harper Collins Publisher, 1991), 112–115; Jane Perlez, "Memo to Schools Chief: A System Adrift," *New York Times*, Jan. 1, 1988, https://www.nytimes.com/1988/01/11/nyregion/memo-to-schools-chief-a-system-adrift.html; Lynell Hancock, review of *Shut Up and Let the Lady Teach: A Teacher's Year in a Public School*, by Emily Sachar," *Los Angeles Times*, July 7, 1991, https://www.latimes.com/archives/la-xpm-1991-07-07-bk-2838-story.html

6. Jane Perlez, "Chaotic State of School Halts Inspection Visit," *New York Times*, Jan. 27, 1988, https://www.nytimes.com/1988/01/27/nyregion/chaotic-state-of-school-halts-inspection-visit.html; Alison Mitchell, "2 Teen-Agers Shot to Death in a Brooklyn School," *New York Times*, Feb. 27, 1992, https://www.nytimes.com/1992/02/27/nyregion/2-teen-agers-shot-to-death-in-a-brooklyn-school.html

7. Nancy Foner, editor, *One Out of Three: Immigrant New York in the Twenty-First Century* (New York: Columbia University Press, 2013), 137–138; Paule Marshall, "Rising Islanders of Bed-Stuy," *New York Times Magazine*, Nov. 3, 1985, https://www.nytimes.com/1985/11/03/magazine/rising-islanders-of-bed-stuy.html

8. Marie Holmes, "Inside the Superintendent's Office: Supt. Vincent Grippo, District 20," *Education Update*, Oct. 2, 2002, http://www.educationupdate.com/archives/2002/oct02/issue/spot-insidethesuper.htm

9. Kay Hymowitz, *The New Brooklyn: What It Takes to Bring a City Back* (Lanham: Rowan & Littlefield, 2017), 51.

10. The Editorial Board, "Opinion: A Principal Problem," *New York Times*, Sept. 17, 1998, https://www.nytimes.com/1998/09/17/opinion/a-principal-problem.html

11. Anemona Hartocollis, "A Rebellion in Red Hook," *New York Newsday*, Dec. 18, 1989, 8.

12. Sean Reardon, *Is Separate Still Unequal? New Evidence on School Segregation and Racial Academic Achievement Gaps* (Stanford: Center for Education Policy Analysis, 2021), https://cepa.stanford.edu/sites/default/files/wp19-06-v092021.pdf

13. Patrick Sharkey, *Neighborhoods and the Black-White Mobility Gap* (Philadelphia: Pew Charitable Trusts, 2009), 11, https://www.pewtrusts.org/-/media/legacy/uploadedfiles/pcs_assets/2009/pewneighborhoods1pdf.pdf

14. Carrie Spector, "School Poverty—Not Racial Composition—Limits Educational Opportunity, According to New Research at Stanford," *Stanford News*,

Sept. 23, 2019, https://news.stanford.edu/2019/09/23/new-data-tool-shows-school-poverty-leads-racial-achievement-gap/

15. Maria Newman, "At New York's Bad Schools, Problem Wasn't Just Money," *The New York Times*, Oct. 25, 1995, https://www.nytimes.com/1995/10/25/nyregion/at-new-york-s-bad-schools-problem-wasn-t-just-money.html

16. Ethan Bronner, "After 45 Years, Resegregation Emerges in Schools, Study Finds," *The New York Times*, June 13, 1999, https://www.nytimes.com/1999/06/13/us/after-45-years-resegregation-emerges-in-schools-study-finds.html

17. Kendra Bischoff and Sean Reardon, *Residential Segregation by Income, 1970–2009*, Russell Sage Foundation, October 16, 2013, https://s4.ad.brown.edu/Projects/Diversity/Data/Report/report10162013.pdf

Chapter 4: The Promise and Pitfalls of School Choice

1. Fabayo McIntosh, interview, "Episode 8: On the Move," School Colors (podcast), Dec. 6, 2019, https://www.schoolcolorspodcast.com/episodes/episode-8-on-the-move

2. Eleanor Randolph, *The Many Lives of Michael Bloomberg* (New York: Simon and Schuster, 2019), 178–179.

3. Elissa Gootman and Robert Gebeloff, "Fewer Children Entering Gifted Programs," *The New York Times*, Oct. 29, 2008, https://www.nytimes.com/2008/10/30/nyregion/30gifted.html

4. Robert Pondisco, *How the Other Half Learns* (New York: Avery, 2019), 331–332; Kate Taylor, "At a Success Academy Charter School, Singling Out Pupils Who Have 'Got to Go,'" *New York Times*, Oct. 29, 2015, https://www.nytimes.com/2015/10/30/nyregion/at-a-success-academy-charter-school-singling-out-pupils-who-have-got-to-go.html; Juan Gonzalez, "Success Charter Network Schools Formally Accused of Violating Rights of Disabled Students," *New York Daily News*, Jan, 20, 2016, https://www.nydailynews.com/new-york/education/success-charter-network-accused-disability-violations-article-1.2503503; Suzanne Popadin, "Success Specializes in Empty Seats: Analysis Shows Moskowitz Schools Fail to Replace Students Who Leave," *New York Teacher*, October 5, 2016, https://www.uft.org/news/news-stories/success-specializes-empty-seats

5. Clara Hemphill, Nicole Mader, and Bruce Cory, *What's Wrong with Math and Science in NYC High Schools?* (New York: Center for New York City Affairs, 2015), 4, https://static1.squarespace.com/static/53ee4f0be4b015b9c3690d84/t/55c413afe4b0a3278e55d9a7/1438913455694/Problems+with+Math+%26+Science+05.pdf

6. Jeff Coplon, "New York State Has the Most-Segregated Schools in the Nation," *New York Magazine*, April 18, 2014, https://nymag.com/news/features/park-slope-collegiate-integration-2014-4/

7. Federal Reserve Bank of New York, "New York City Spending per Student," https://www.newyorkfed.org/data-and-statistics/data-visualization/nyc-school-spending#interactive/overview

8. Norm Fruchter and Christina Mokhatar, "New York School Segregation, Then and Now," in *Racial Inequality in New York City Since 1965*, ed. Benjamin P. Bowser (Albany: SUNY Press, 2019), 64–65.

9. Jim Dwyer, "The Impossible Mayor of the Possible," *New York Times*, Aug. 16, 2013, https://www.nytimes.com/2013/08/18/nyregion/the-impossible-mayor-of-the-possible.html

10. Jonathan Mahler, "New York Is Back. Now It Has a Second Chance," *New York Times Magazine*, June 8, 2021, https://www.nytimes.com/interactive/2021/06/08/magazine/nyc-inequality.html

11. David W. Chen, "Annotations on a Speech," *New York Times*, Oct. 3, 2013, https://archive.nytimes.com/www.nytimes.com/interactive/2013/10/04/nyregion/deblasio-abny-speech.html

Chapter 5: How Gentrification Brought Conflict

1. Shaila Dewan, interview, "Episode 7: New Kids on the Block," School Colors (podcast), Nov. 22, 2019, https://www.schoolcolorspodcast.com/episodes/episode-7-new-kids-on-the-block

2. Lance Freeman, *There Goes the 'Hood: Views of Gentrification from the Ground Up* (Philadelphia: Temple University Press, 2016), 56, 229.

3. NYU Furman Center, *State of New York City's Housing and Neighborhoods in 2018* (New York: NYU Furman Center, 2018), 54.

4. Freeman, 2 60, 111, 121.

5. Eve L. Ewing, *Ghosts in the Schoolyard: Racism and School Closings on Chicago's South Side* (Chicago: University of Chicago Press, 2018), 47.

6. Kate Taylor, "Race and Class Collide in a Plan for Two Brooklyn Schools," *New York Times*, Sept. 22, 2015, https://www.nytimes.com/2015/09/23/nyregion/race-and-class-collide-in-a-plan-for-two-brooklyn-schools.html

7. Clara Hemphill, *Five Steps to Integrate New York City's Elementary Schools* (New York: Center for New York City Affairs, 2016), 6, http://www.centernyc.org/five-steps-to-integrate-elementary-schools

8. Natasha Seaton, interview, "Episode 7: New Kids on the Block," School Colors (podcast), Nov. 22, 2019, https://www.schoolcolorspodcast.com/episodes/episode-7-new-kids-on-the-block

9. Marlon Rice, "The Drama in District 16," *Our Time Press*, July 2018, https://ourtimepress.com/the-drama-in-district-16/

10. Cieanne Everett, interview, "Episode 1: Old School," School Colors (podcast), Sept. 20, 2019, https://www.schoolcolorspodcast.com/episodes/episode-1-old-school

Chapter 6: Bringing the Community Together

1. Joshua Goodman et al., *Heat and Learning* (Cambridge: National Bureau of Economic Research, 2018), https://www.nber.org/papers/w24639; Alvin Chang, "How the US Lets Hot School Days Sabotage Learning," *The Guardian*, June 10, 2021, https://www.theguardian.com/us-news/2021/jun/10/hot-school-days-heat-learning-data-us

2. Amy Zimmer, "Here's Why Schools Have a Hard Time Getting Classrooms Air-Conditioned," *DNAinfo*, July 28, 2016, https://www.dnainfo.com/new-york/20160728/upper-west-side/heres-why-schools-have-hard-time-getting-classrooms-air-conditioned/

3. D. H. Locke, B. Hall, J. M. Grove, et al., "Residential Housing Segregation and Urban Tree Canopy in 37 US Cities," *Npj Urban Sustain* 1, 15 (2021), https://doi.org/10.1038/s42949-021-00022-0; Emily Badger, "How Redlining's Racist Effects Lasted for Decades," *New York Times*, Aug. 24, 2017, https://www.nytimes.com/2017/08/24/upshot/how-redlinings-racist-effects-lasted-for-decades.html

4. New York City Health Department, *Environmental & Health Data Portal, Heath Vulnerability Index*, 2018, https://a816-dohbesp.nyc.gov/IndicatorPublic/VisualizationData.aspx?id=2191,4466a0,100,Summarize

5. The official website of New York City, "Mayor de Blasio, Chancellor Fariña and City Council Announce Every Classroom Will Have Air Conditioning by 2022," news release, April 25, 2017, https://www1.nyc.gov/office-of-the-mayor/news/261-17/mayor-de-blasio-chancellor-fari-a-city-council-every-classroom-will-have-air

6. A. T. Geronimus, M. T. Hicken, J. A. Pearson, et al., "Do US Black Women Experience Stress-Related Accelerated Biological Aging?" *Hum Nat* 21, 19–38 (2010). https://doi.org/10.1007/s12110-010-9078-0

Chapter 7: Problems Outside the School's Control

1. Hedy N. Chang and Mariajosé Romero, *Present, Engaged, and Accounted For: The Critical Importance of Addressing Chronic Absence in the Early Grades* (New York: National Center for Children in Poverty, 2008), http://www.nccp.org/wp-content/uploads/2008/09/text_837.pdf; Linda S. Olson, *Why September*

Matters: Improving Student Attendance (Baltimore: Baltimore Education Research Coalition, 2014), http://baltimore-berc.org/wp-content/uploads/2014/08/SeptemberAttendanceBriefJuly2014.pdf

2. Institute for Children, Poverty, and Homelessness, *The High Stakes of Low Wages: Employment among New York City's Homeless Parents* (New York: 2013), https://www.icphusa.org/reports/3884/

3. Jane Sundius and Martha Farneth, *Missing School: The Epidemic of School Absence* (Baltimore: Open Society Foundations, 2008), 11, https://www.opensocietyfoundations.org/publications/missing-school-epidemic-school-absence#publications_download

4. R. Balfanz and V. Byrnes, *The Importance of Being in School: A Report on Absenteeism in the Nation's Public Schools* (Baltimore: Johns Hopkins University Center for Social Organization of Schools, 2012), 3, https://new.every1graduates.org/wp-content/uploads/2012/05/FINALChronicAbsenteeismReport_May16.pdf

5. New York City Health Department, *Community Health Profiles: Brooklyn Community District 3, Bedford Stuyvesant*, 2015, https://www1.nyc.gov/assets/doh/downloads/pdf/data/2015chp-bk3.pdf

6. Kristen Lewis, Sarah Burd-Sharps, and Bruce Cory, *Public Housing and Asthma: Another Winter of Discontent, or Relief at Last?* (New York: Center for New York City Affairs, 2019), http://www.centernyc.org/public-housing-and-asthma; Dan Goldberg, "The Long-Term Health Consequences of Living at NYCHA," *Politico*, April 9, 2018, https://www.politico.com/states/new-york/albany/story/2018/04/06/the-long-term-health-consequences-of-living-at-nycha-352931

7. Advocates for Children, *New Data Show Number of NYC Students Who Are Homeless Topped 100,000 for Fourth Consecutive Year*, news release, Oct. 28, 2019, https://www.advocatesforchildren.org/node/1403

8. National Academies of Sciences, Engineering, and Medicine, *Permanent Supportive Housing: Evaluating the Evidence for Improving Health Outcomes Among People Experiencing Chronic Homelessness* (Washington, DC: The National Academies Press, 2018), Appendix B, https://doi.org/10.17226/25133; Furman Center for Real Estate and Urban Policy, *Housing Policy in New York City: A Brief History* (New York: Furman Center, 2006), https://furmancenter.org/research/publication/housing-policy-in-new-york-city-a-brief-history; Coalition for the Homeless, *Why Are So Many People Homeless?* (New York: Coalition for the Homeless, 2021), https://www.coalitionforthehomeless.org/why-are-so-many-people-homeless/

9. Matthew Desmond, *Evicted: Poverty and Profit in the American City* (New York: Broadway Books, 2016), 4.

10. Kim Nauer et al., *Strengthening Schools by Strengthening Families: Community Strategies to Reverse Chronic Absenteeism in the Early Grades and Improve*

Supports for Children and Families (New York: Center for New York City Affairs, 2008), 11, https://www.attendanceworks.org/wp-content/uploads/2015/01/Strengthening-Schools-by-Strengthening-Families-Oct-2008.pdf

11. Tara Kini and Anne Podolsky, *Does Teaching Experience Increase Teacher Effectiveness? A Review of the Research* (Palo Alto, CA: Learning Policy Institute, 2016), https://learningpolicyinstitute.org/product/does-teaching-experience-increase-teacher-effectiveness-review-research

12. Linn Posey-Maddox, *When Middle-Class Parents Choose Urban Schools: Class, Race & the Challenge of Equity in Public Education* (Chicago: University of Chicago Press, 2014), 3.

13. New York State Department of Health, *Residential Fires Disproportionately Impact Vulnerable Populations*, 2014, https://www.health.ny.gov/prevention/injury_prevention/children/toolkits/fire/residential_fires_impact_vunerable_populations.htm; New York City Health Department, *Community Health Profiles: Brooklyn Community District 3, Bedford Stuyvesant*, 2015, 5, https://www1.nyc.gov/assets/doh/downloads/pdf/data/2015chp-bk3.pdf

Chapter 8: COVID-19 Tests the Community

1. *The New York Times*, "Tracking Coronavirus in New York: Latest Map and Case Count," https://www.nytimes.com/interactive/2021/us/new-york-covid-cases.html

2. Hannah Kuchler and Andrew Edgecliffe-Johnson, "How New York's Missteps Let COVID-19 Overwhelm the US," *Financial Times*, Oct. 22, 2020, https://www.ft.com/content/a52198f6-0d20-4607-b12a-05110bc48723

3. J. David Goodman, "How Delays and Unheeded Warnings Hindered New York's Virus Fight," *New York Times*, April 8, 2020, https://www.nytimes.com/2020/04/08/nyregion/new-york-coronavirus-response-delays.html; Shant Shahrigian, "De Blasio slams former NYC Health Commissioner Dr. Barbot following her interview on BBC, *New York Daily News*, March 10, 2021, https://www.nydailynews.com/coronavirus/ny-nyc-covid-barbot-de-blasio-criticism-20210310-4tpdhdbpyrfcdc7wewrq5huida-story.html

4. Larry Buchanan, Quoctrung Bui, and Jugal K. Patel, "Black Lives Matter May Be the Largest Movement in U.S. History," *New York Times*, July 3, 2020, https://www.nytimes.com/interactive/2020/07/03/us/george-floyd-protests-crowd-size.html

5. Ali Watkins, "An Unprepared N.Y.P.D. Badly Mishandled Floyd Protests, Watchdog Says," *New York Times*, Dec. 18, 2020, https://www.nytimes.com/2020/12/18/nyregion/nypd-george-floyd-protests.html

6. Michael Gold, "Two Teenagers Are Among 8 Killed on Deadly Day in New York City," *New York Times*, July 27, 2020, https://www.nytimes.com/2020/07/27/nyregion/nyc-shootings-weekend.html

7. Ashley Southall, "2 Men Charged in Killing of 1-Year-Old Boy at Brooklyn Cookout," *New York Times*, May 6, 2021, https://www.nytimes.com/2021/05/06/nyregion/dashawn-austin-charged-davell-gardner.html

8. Ashley Southall, "Shootings Have Soared. Is the N.Y.P.D. Pulling Back?" *New York Times*, July 16, 2020, https://www.nytimes.com/2020/07/16/nyregion/nyc-shootings-nypd.html

9. Rocco Parascandola, "As gunplay soars, busts and tickets fall dramatically," *New York Daily News*, July 17, 2020, 11.

10. Patrick Sharkey, Amy Ellen Schwartz, Ingrid Gould Ellen, and Johanna Lacoe, "High Stakes in the Classroom, High Stakes on the Street: The Effects of Community Violence on Students' Standardized Test Performance," *Sociological Science* 1: 199–220 (2014) DOI: 10.15195/v1.a14

11. Andrew Bacher-Hicks and Elijah de la Campa, *Social Costs of Proactive Policing: The Impact of NYC's Stop and Frisk Program on Educational Atainment,* Work. Pap., Kennedy Sch. Gov., Harv. Univ., Cambridge, 2020, https://drive.google.com/file/d/1sSxhfmDY3N1VAN5XwyRObE65tmAZzhTj/view

12. Joscha Legewie and Jeffrey Fagan, "Aggressive Policing and the Educational Performance of Minority Youth," *American Sociological Review*, 82–84, 220–247, 2019, https://journals.sagepub.com/doi/full/10.1177/0003122419826020

13. *The New York Times*, "Tracking Coronavirus in New York City, N.Y.: Latest Map and Case Count," https://www.nytimes.com/interactive/2021/us/new-york-city-new-york-covid-cases.html

Chapter 9: "Trust Is the Glue"

1. Alex Zimmerman and Thomas Wilburn, "75% of NYC Public Schools Enrolled Fewer Students This Year. Here's a Breakdown of Every School," *Chalkbeat*, Jan. 28, 2022, https://ny.chalkbeat.org/2022/1/28/22907058/nyc-school-level-enrollment-decline-search?utm_

2. Reema Amin, "NYC Schools to Get Billions of New Dollars Under State Budget Deal," *Chalkbeat*, April 7, 2021, https://ny.chalkbeat.org/2021/4/7/22372087/nyc-schools-to-get-billions-of-new-dollars-under-state-budget-deal

3. Anthony S. Bryk and Barbara Schneider, *Trust in Schools: A Core Resource for Improvement* (New York: Russell Sage Foundation, 2002).

Chapter 10: The Work Still to Be Done

1. Mimi Engel, Robin Jacob, Amy Claessens, and Anna Erickson, "Kindergarten in a Large Urban District," *Educational Researcher* 50, no. 6 (August 2021): 401–415. https://doi.org/10.3102/0013189X211041586

2. S. B. Neuman, T. Kaefer, and A. M. Pinkham, "A Double Dose of Disadvantage: Language Experiences for Low-Income Children in Home and School." *Journal*

of Educational Psychology, 110(1), 102–118 (2018) https://doi.org/10.1037/edu0000201

3. Lisa Delpit, *Other People's Children: Cultural Conflict in the Classroom* (New York: New Press, 1995), 11–20.

Conclusion

1. New York City Independent Budget Office, *How Has Public School Enrollment Changed Two Years Into the Covid-19 Pandemic?* (New York: July 2022), https://www.ibo.nyc.ny.us/iboreports/how-has-public-school-enrollment-changed-two-years-into-the-covid-19-pandemic-nycbtn-july2022.html

2. Clara Hemphill, Nicole Mader, and the InsideSchools Staff, *Integrated Schools in a Segregated City: 10 Strategies that Have Made New York City Elementary Schools More Diverse* (New York: Center for New York City Affairs, 2016), http://www.centernyc.org/integrated-schools-segregated-city

3. School Diversity Advisory Group, *Making the Grade: The Path to Real Integration and Equity for NYC Public School Students* (New York, 2019), https://docs.wixstatic.com/ugd/1c478c_4de7a85cae884c53a8d48750e0858172.pdf7

4. New York City Council, *School Diversity in NYC: Making Sure Our City's Schools Reflect the Diversity of Its Residents Is a Top Priority*, https://council.nyc.gov/data/school-diversity-in-nyc

5. Raj Chetty, John N. Friedman, and Jonah Rockoff, "New Evidence on the Long-Term Impacts of Tax Credits," *Proceedings. Annual Conference on Taxation and Minutes of the Annual Meeting of the National Tax Association* 104 (2011): 116–24. http://www.jstor.org/stable/prancotamamnta.104.116

6. Heather C. McGhee, *The Sum of Us: What Racism Costs Everyone and How We Can Prosper Together* (New York: One World, 2021), 179.

Data Sources

Data on school enrollment, test scores, racial and ethnic breakdown, absenteeism, and the proportion of low-income and homeless children in individual schools comes from the independent nonprofit InsideSchools.org website (which I founded); the New York State Education Department (NYSED); the New York City Department of Education; and IntegrateNY.org, a website by Margardy Research built with NYSED data.

IntegrateNY.org has enrollment data for each school by race and grade level from 1978 to the present. InsideSchools (insideschools.org) has profiles of each of the city's schools, with data drawn from the state education data site (https://data.nysed.gov/) and the city's education website (https://infohub.nyced.org/reports/school-quality/information-and-data-overview).

A Word About Names

A word about names: Parents at Brighter Choice call one another by their first names—Keesha, Keyonn, Talia, Ibrahim, and Frances—and, on second reference, I've used their first names in the text. The parents call staff members by their last names—Mr. Daniel, Ms. Nunes, Ms. Brown—and I've used their last names on second reference here. The parent coordinator (both a staff member and a parent) uses her first name plus an honorific—Ms. Deittra, as she is called here. In this way, I've tried to re-create the atmosphere of the school as seen through parents' eyes.

Index

About the Author

Clara Hemphill, founding editor of InsideSchools.org, is a lifelong journalist who has built a career helping New York City parents navigate a complex system of school choice. She is the author of *New York City's Best Public Pre-K and Elementary Schools, New York City's Best Public Middle Schools,* and *New York City's Best Public High Schools.* She was a foreign correspondent for *The Associated Press,* a producer for *CBS News* in Rome, and a reporter and editorial writer for *New York Newsday,* where she shared the Pulitzer Prize for local reporting. She led a team of researchers at The New School's Center for New York City Affairs that produced policy reports on increasing racial and socioeconomic integration of the city's schools. She was a visiting journalist at the Russell Sage Foundation, where she completed research for this book. Her son and daughter, now grown, attended public schools in Manhattan and the Bronx. She lives in Manhattan with her husband.

Printed and bound by CPI Group (UK) Ltd, Croydon, CR0 4YY

09/06/2025

14685975-0001